Mum had a Kingswood

Mum had a Kingswood

Tales from the life and mind of ROSSO

TIM ROSS

ALLEN&UNWIN

First published in 2010

Allen & Unwin
83 Alexander Street
Crows Nest NSW 2065
Australia
Phone: (61 2) 8425 0100
Fax: (61 2) 9906 2218
Email: info@allenandunwin.com
Web: www.allenandunwin.com

Cataloguing-in-Publication details are available
from the National Library of Australia
www.librariesaustralia.nla.gov.au

ISBN 978 1 74237 507 6

Cover design by Luke Causby, Blue Cork
Internal design by Darian Causby, Highway 51
Typeset in 12.5/20pt Bembo by Kirby Jones
Printed in Australia by McPherson's Printing Group

10 9 8 7 6 5 4 3 2 1

Mixed Sources

Product group from well-managed
forests, and other controlled sources
www.fsc.org Cert no. SGS-COC-004121
© 1996 Forest Stewardship Council

The paper in this book is FSC certified.
FSC promotes environmentally responsible,
socially beneficial and economically viable
management of the world's forests.

CONTENTS

Part 3

Part 4

Part 5

Part 6

Stuff:

Part 7

The bit at the beginning

I found myself in a bookstore recently and after five minutes of searching I realised that there wasn't a single book featuring stories about my life on the shelves. Why on earth hasn't Alain de Botton punched out *The Philosophies of Tim 'Rosso' Ross*? Inspired by what seemed to be a startlingly large gap in the market I have decided to write a book to address this situation. Starting with my own wide-ranging brief, which I classified as 'Stuff I Reckon Is Funny', the journey of writing this book has made me incredibly nostalgic about things that happened when I was a kid, when, dare I say it, things were simpler. Back in the day, we sure as hell didn't walk around with shit in a plastic bag when we took the dog for a walk.

When I thought about it, I remembered some very funny stories that range from growing up in the suburbs in the 1970s and '80s and then from my university days living in share houses and playing in bands in the '90s.

I've also included a bunch of stories about the celebrities I've encountered over the years—what's it like to have John Travolta pat you like you're a labrador, have a fight about the definition of 'chick flick' with Cameron Diaz, or embarrass yourself in the home of an Academy Award-winning actor? On top of that, there are pages of weird, wonderful, absurd and ridiculous ... stuff, which I reckon is funny.

After eleven years of doing three hours of radio a day, a fantastic medium but one that is truly disposable, one where your work goes up in the air and disappears forever, it's been a joy to work on something far more tangible. It's something I'm incredibly proud of.

It's also going to be bloody handy to keep next to the dunny so I can fill in the gaps in my life when I get old and lose me marbles.

All the best and I hope you enjoy.

Rosso

PART

1

1
Mum's old green Kingswood

I have a soft spot for Australia's car culture, especially for cars made here in the 1970s.

Last year I was walking down Church Street in Parramatta, and I stopped at a JB HiFi store where they had a TV in the window playing the 1977 Bathurst 1000 on DVD. I was riveted and so were others as a crowd gathered like it was 1956 and we were watching the Olympics in a shopfront window because we didn't have a TV at home. When the Ford team of Allan Moffatt and

5

Colin Bond went over the line in their famous 1, 2 finish, the vision cut to the view from Channel 7's overhead chopper of these two hulking Ford XCs crossing the line. A wave of nostalgia-tinged excitement gripped the half a dozen strangers who had been drawn to watch this classic race. We smiled at each other, exchanged a few 'How good was that?'-type comments, and then went on with our business, our lives just a little brighter all because of some old footage of a car race more than thirty years ago.

When Mum bought her Kingswood in 1975, there was pandemonium in our household. My brothers and I were out of minds with excitement. We climbed all over that six-cylinder, big four-door sedan, checking out the glove box, sliding across the bench seat and admiring the shape of this car that just seemed so modern. Mum had pretty much always had Holdens, but it wasn't due to any loyalty in a Holden vs Ford rivalry kind of way; this latest car turned up in the driveway because a family friend worked at Holden and Mum got a great deal. I think she got it for a steal because it was a ghastly shade of lime green with a cream vinyl interior.

Not long after its arrival at Wooralla Drive, Mount Eliza, Mum and Dad took us to Adelaide for a holiday. With three boys piled in the back, we took off across the country. As the temperature hit the mid thirties, Mum turned round and yelled at us to put our seatbelts on. Dehydrated (this was the '70s, remember; no-one drank water then) we explained to Mum that the polymers in our polyester velour jumpers had moulded with the vinyl seat in the car and so we didn't need seatbelts because we weren't going anywhere.

Despite our love of Mum's new Kingswood, we were too young at the time to realise some of the deficiencies of Holden engineering. The HJ Kingswood didn't exactly handle like a dream; in fact they were never used as police cars for this very reason. In the early '90s I went along to show some support for my old mate Bulldog, who had a small driving misdemeanour matter being decided at the local magistrates court. Before his case, a bloke had been charged with reckless and unlicensed driving of a Holden Kingswood while he was twice the legal limit. When the magistrate asked the police prosecutor whether the defendant had made any excuse for his behaviour on being arrested, the officer read from his notebook in a classically deadpan manner, 'He said. "You try driving this piece of shit when you're pissed, officer!"'

One of the stranger design features of the Kingswood was that the fuel cap was placed behind the rear numberplate. To access the tank you had to pull the hinged numberplate down to reveal the cap. In those days, most petrol stations had full driveway service so as we pulled up halfway to Adelaide, my brothers and I giggled at the comic possibilities of the guy at the servo walking around the car, scratching his head, damned if he could work out where to put the petrol. As we stopped at the bowser, the three of us waited in anticipation as the crusty old attendant came over and Dad wound down the window and said, 'Fill her up with super, please'. Without missing a beat the bloke walked round the back of the car, lifted up the numberplate and dutifully filled the tank up with super. We were amazed; I'm not sure that three boys under ten could understand that the Kingswood was actually the most popular car in the country at the time.

It seemed like we spent half our lives in that car. Mum, a doctor, used to pick us up from school, and then pop into the hospital to check on some patients on our way home. To keep ourselves occupied we would dare each other to take the car out of park, release the handbrake, and see how far we were prepared to let the car roll before chickening out and quickly hitting the brakes to avoid rolling into a surgeon's Mercedes. Only marginally less dangerous than that was when we got a box of Kleenex out of the glove box and set fire to individual tissues with the cigarette lighter.

When I was seven, we went and stayed at a family friend's beach house. Mum and I went a night earlier than Dad and my brothers, and when we arrived at the old fibro shack Mum turned into the driveway and hit a rock sticking out of the lawn with one of the tyres. It caused the Kingswood to launch into the air and land, wedging the garden tap underneath the front bumper bar. This was quite a concern because we were trapped; any attempt to move the car would mean snapping the water pipe. What was *more* troubling was that Mum had promised me a Chiko Roll and that wasn't going to happen anytime soon if we couldn't drive to the shops. Somehow I came up with a brilliant solution. I got the jack out of the boot of the car, jacked up the front of the car until the car was clear of the tap and pipe and then got Mum to start the ignition, slam the vehicle in reverse and drive off the jack—and the tap. Despite Mum's scepticism of my ingenious plan, it worked: the car slid off the jack, missed the tap, completely fucked the lawn, and I got a deep-fried snack.

In the early 1980s, Mum upgraded to a green Holden Commodore with a green vinyl interior, and Dad started driving the Kingswood. Dad was now not only driving Mum's car but he had taken to wearing an old pair of her sunglasses too. Dad has what is best described as a light afro, so it wasn't a surprise that on the day he picked us up after seeing *Ghostbusters* my mates jumped into the back of the car and said, 'Hi, Mrs Ross!'

In the hands of the old man the beast had some trying times. Because Dad was an antiques dealer, he added some roof racks and channelled a Balinese family on a motorbike with the amount of stuff he could tie on the roof. One of the best things I ever saw was him coming up the driveway, forgetting he had a nineteenth-century wardrobe on top of the car, and barrelling straight into the carport. I watched the car go in, but the wardrobe didn't make the clearance. It hit the front board and took the roof racks clean off the car, and then landed directly behind the car like something out of a Road Runner cartoon.

His best modification to the Kingswood was when the lock to the boot seized. This sent Dad into a panic because the boot was filled to the brim with an assortment of shit that he'd just bought at auction. Rather than take it somewhere to be fixed, he just got Gary from next door to come over with his angle grinder. With some help from my oldest brother Steve, they took the back seat out of the car, Gary fired up the angle grinder and, under Dad's instruction, cut a square hole 2 feet by 2 feet through the body of the car so we could dive in and remove his precious cargo. Now you don't have to be an automotive engineer to work out that removing such a large piece of the car was going to affect its structural integrity, and Dad soon found that the back doors would fly open when he went round a roundabout at any speed over 20 kilometres an hour.

Unfortunately the old girl didn't have much time left on the clock, and a week after Steve drove us down the road to the Dromana Drive-In and we sat on her bonnet to watch local legends Australian Crawl do their very last gig, her head gasket blew and she was off to the wreckers for 150 bucks.

2
Our house: A story of survival

The way my brothers and I treated it, the house we grew up in could have withstood Hurricane Katrina. In the late '70s Mum and Dad renovated it to give us all a room for ourselves. What this did in the process was extend the hallway and give us some extra room for corridor cricket. Although this sport was banned, it didn't stop us from us spending hours on school holidays battering a tennis ball and the walls in equal measure. When we heard Mum or Dad come up the driveway we'd have to quickly hide the bat and ball in Stephen's room and pretend we'd been doing homework, watching TV or reading.

One afternoon we had the stereo on extra loud and hadn't heard Mum come home from work early. It wasn't until the last moment, when the front door closed, that we had to scatter. Stephen took the bat into his room, I ducked into the bathroom with the tennis ball and Campbell dived onto the couch picking up what he thought was his Robert Ludlum novel. It wasn't until Mum asked him if he was enjoying his book that he realised he'd picked up Mum's copy of *Everywoman* by mistake. It would have been even funnier if Mum offered him a mirror to examine himself.

Obviously indoor sports were forbidden because of the damage they did to the house but some impromptu sports were impossible to ban. When Wiltshire introduced the nifty StaySharp knife in the 1970s they were pretty damn fancy. Their ability to stay sharp had an unexpected use when I chucked one in a fit of rage at my brother, who thankfully ducked, and it wedged half way in the pine-clad wall. It took us ten minutes to remove and left a hole in the wall that we never managed to explain.

There was far worse to come when Steve started mucking around with the ignition of Dad's little Suzuki soft-top 4WD and managed to drive the car straight into the side of the house. Mum, who was upstairs making dinner at the time, thought we'd suffered an almighty earthquake. Despite a little bit of damage to the front side panel of the car and the bull bar, the little jeep was actually okay. The house had moved several centimetres permanently and the bricks were cracked. My brother, despite being only thirteen, was saddled with the shame of being a 'fucked driver'.

I decided to go one better when I was thirteen (a very unlucky number for our household). Mum had a very strict rationing of Prima Orange Juice drinks (the ones that most people call 'poppers' these days) and I decided I'd tuck into one without permission. Rather than dispose of the evidence in the bin, I took the opportunity to go downstairs into Dad's workshop, which was inside, directly below Campbell's room. There I created a diorama/installation featuring the crushed container and a few small plastic army men on Dad's workbench. Once they were looking decidedly arty/*Guns of Navarone*-ish I poured a bit of paint stripper over them and lit the diorama with a match. With a small flame going I ramped up the Napalm stakes and poured more of the paint stripper straight from the tin directly onto the flame.

I don't think I need Dr Julius Sumner Miller to return from the grave to tell you what happened next.

The moment the liquid hit the flames, they flew skyward and set the wall and the roof on fire. Petrified, I stood there screaming as the flames licked the walls.

Luckily Campbell took my screams as a sign to take a break from watching *Wide World of Sports* and come down, find a hose from outside and put out the fire before it took the whole house down.

Not only had I destroyed Dad's workshop, there was water everywhere. This was going to be a hard one to blame on the dog when the folks got home.

The other near scrape for the house was when a tree fell on the roof in a storm. Luckily it only caused a small hole the size of a 50-cent piece and Dad had me up there scraping the asbestos roof with a wire brush to prepare the surface so I could fill it with a plastic filler.

Mucking around with asbestos, now those were the days.

3
Mixed lollies

When I was a kid I used to ride my bike everywhere—and almost killed myself in the process on numerous occasions. One of the coolest things I loved to do on my Malvern Star racer was cycle with my hands off the handlebars. I used to watch all the older boys do it, so once I perfected it I was pretty damn pleased with myself.

One day I went down to the shops to buy some mixed lollies and some Whizz Fizz. With my lollies in my duffle coat pocket, I was very smoothly dipping the small plastic spoon into the fizz while riding my bike along. It was fine until I looked down at the bag for just too long and barrelled into a woman walking along with her shopping. I'd actually managed to steer the bike between her legs, and when I felt the bike wobble I looked up to find her holding on to the handlebars. I dropped the Whizz Fizz instinctively and steadied the bike. For five metres or so I carried the woman along until I hit the kerb and we both fell sideways. A bit shaken, I quickly apologised and helped her pick up her groceries and, despite me almost killing her, she felt sorry for me. So this woman of forty-two asked me back to her house for a cup of tea and a piece of cake, and then she promptly seduced me and made me a man …Yeah right, what actually happened was she went off her nut, calling me irresponsible and a reckless idiot, and wanted me to pay for her damaged groceries. Given I had five cents on me at the time that wasn't going to wash, so I got back on my bike and headed off to avoid any further tirade.

On school holidays my brothers and I would cycle round the neighbourhood knocking on people's doors to see whether they had any odd jobs that needed doing for a bit of spare cash. We'd rake up leaves or wash cars for an hour, and end up with 50 cents each. Afterwards we'd head straight down to the milk bar and stock up.

Mum had a Kingswood

When we knocked on one door, the woman put us to work raking up all the leaves in her rather large backyard as well as cutting a large stack of wood with a small bandsaw. It looked like it would be a good half day's work. After we'd been toiling away for an hour, the woman came out the back and told us she was out for the rest of the day and gave us 20 cents to finish the job ... between us! We were pretty incensed by the tight-arsed nature of the offering but decided to do the right thing and finish off the job anyway.

As soon as she'd backed her Datsun out of the driveway my brother called us round to the side of the house. While he'd been stacking the wood he'd noticed a crate of empty 1-litre soft drink bottles. At the time these bottles were recycled—not in a crush and melt them down again kind of way, but washed and reused by the manufacturers. As a result when you returned them to the milk bar you'd get 20 cents per bottle. Ever the mathematician, my brother did the sums and before you knew it we'd downed tools, the crate was on the front of his bike, and we were headed down the shops with $2.40 worth of bottles. That got us bags of mixed lollies, Freddo Frogs, White Knights, Choo Choo Bars, a mountain of hot chips and a can of creaming soda each.

It was at this visit to the milk bar that we worked out that after we gave the owner the returnable bottles, he took them out the back of his shop and left them by his backdoor. After we'd finished what we could eat of our feast, my brothers hoisted me over the fence and I stealthily passed our recently returned bottles—plus a few more—over the fence to my brothers' eagerly waiting hands. Then we hid them in the bushes for a couple of days before taking them back to the milk bar to collect our bounty again. The owner was none the wiser. It was the perfect crime.

The word got out about this opportunity and it seemed that everyone we knew was in on the scam. Today in my memory I can see us all jumping over the fence in our Golden Breed windcheaters and Amco Rider jeans like an old silent movie with 'The Entertainer' from *The Sting* being played underneath it.

Like all great scams, someone pushed it too far. One of my brother's mates, Jimmy, jumped the fence, took a case, walked into the shop and got his refund. He then jumped the fence again, grabbed the bottles and went straight back into the shop and tried to get the refund. By this stage, unsurprisingly, the shopkeeper had been getting suspicious of these hordes of kids bringing in bottles only to have them disappear from out the back. So, unbeknownst to Jimmy he'd decided use a red Texta to put a mark on the top of the bottles to catch the crims! Jimmy was caught red-handed and our scam was over for good.

This wasn't the last of Jimmy's problems. Not long after, he fronted up at our place with a paper bag full of fireworks. We weren't allowed to have fireworks so we were out of our minds with excitement, and off we rushed to the adjoining bush to set them off. Jimmy mostly had baby rockets; generally you'd put the stem in a Coke bottle, light the fuse, stand back and watch them go skyward.

We didn't have a bottle, however, so for some bizarre reason Jimmy improvised and decided to pull down his pants and use his bottom as a convenient Coke bottle substitute. We of course thought this was hilarious until things went horribly wrong when the rocket didn't ignite as forcefully as expected, and the flame scalded his arse, fizzled out and fell to the ground. With Jimmy screaming in pain and his pants around his ankles we all ran back home where he faced the indignity of having to lie on the couch in front of all of us as Mum applied Savlon to his blistered ring. Not long after, fireworks were banned in the state of Victoria. We blamed Jimmy.

Our lounge room, with its black modular Featherston couch, was a makeshift surgery for Mum. It's where she would remove stitches, examine sprains and bruises, or other interventions. On one particular occasion, I was quietly sitting there, watching *Simon Townsend's Wonderworld*, when I felt Mum doing something weird to my arm. Before I knew it, she'd jabbed a needle in my arm and given me a tetanus shot.

When we were younger, before we started doing odd jobs, our other trick was to go and visit any old people around the neighbourhood under the pretence of being friendly—but really we were just hoping they'd give us some lollies and biscuits. Can you imagine that today? Kids of six or seven just knocking on people's doors to say 'Hi!' Like home delivery for paedophiles. The oldies were pretty nice to us, and we thought we were so sneaky just rocking up, eating their goodies and then leaving as soon as we'd knocked off half a dozen Monte Carlos.

Karma got the better of me, though. One day, after I'd been feigning interest in some old duck's patchwork while I munched on Chocolate Royals, I bumped into some girls slightly older than me, who lived around the corner. While I was boasting to them about the number of biscuits I'd managed to con out of the old lady, the girls' red setter started mounting me and humping my leg. Within seconds it had knocked me over and continued to molest me until I started crying, begging them to get it off me. I finally managed to push the dog away and ran home, humiliated.

The old man was a great inventor when we were kids. He built us a cubby that had a drawbridge and a ladder leading up a turret with a hinged manhole at the top that you could open up and look out over the top of our house and across the Moorooduc plains. He also built a flying fox out the back of our house that stretched 50 metres down a steep hill. Hung between two large gums, the flying fox had a large basket that resembled a hot air balloon's gondola. We'd all pile into it and rocket down the hill before the pulley would hit a large rope stopper just a metre before the tree. The force from the impact would throw the basket at a 90 degree angle, almost scattering us onto the ground about 8 metres below. I remember it being a terrifying ride, and Dad took it out of commission for safety reasons sometime around 1976. At a time when kids rode bikes without helmets, knocked on strangers' doors, and shoved firecrackers up their jacksies, that flying fox must have been bloody dangerous for us to stop using it.

Dad also made us fantastic billycarts out of old pram wheels, golf carts and anything else he had lying around. We'd create jumps out of bricks and large pieces of plywood. Barrelling down the hill, we'd become airborne over a jump, fly off the side, scrape the bejesus out of our knees and elbows, then dust ourselves off and do it all over again, pausing only to put some Penetrine on the axles to keep the wheels rolling smoothly and some Mercurochrome on our wounds to keep us firing on all cylinders. It's amazing how I probably used that stuff once a week when I was a kid, but haven't used it for twenty years. Mind you I did read the other day that Mercurochrome hasn't been available in the US since 1998 due to fears about mercury poisoning. Given they started using it in 1919, it took them a while to work that one out.

One day we decided that we would jump over this kid, Gareth, who lived up the road. Gareth wasn't the smartest kid going round; he'd developed a little set of boy boobies because he ate vanilla slices for breakfast. He'd once turned up with what he claimed was a new pet guinea pig he'd found in his backyard. It wasn't exactly a guinea pig but more like a manky rat.

Anyway, we positioned Gareth behind the jump and my brother took an extra long run-up and came hurtling down the hill. Unfortunately the pin holding the wheel to the back axle snapped halfway down the makeshift runway and my brother, battling to keep control of his vehicle on only three wheels, missed the jump completely and rammed straight into Gareth's head. I'm sure he had a mild case of concussion but we bought his silence with a bowl of Neapolitan ice cream sprinkled with Milo.

As the years went by, the urban sprawl started its push into our neighbourhood and the bush became building sites, which were great places to play after school and on weekends. Builders always left *Australasian Post* or *People* magazines in the site dunnies, and we would brave the stench to grab them.

Boys being boys we'd often do a bit of vandalism, pushing over bricks or kicking a plaster wall. One afternoon we were riding around on our bikes and we stopped at a house where all the neighbourhood kids had been visiting and making mischief. I'd found a small tack hammer by the side of the road and I had it in my hand when I was jumping across the floor beams of the house. As I balanced on the joists, the owner jumped out from behind a partially built brick wall and grabbed me. 'So it's you whose been knocking over my bricks, is it?' I pleaded ignorance and played one of my great school kid cards—if in doubt, pretend to be slightly retarded—and convinced him that I just liked playing at being a carpenter and of course I'd only hammer nails that were in the wood and I would never ever push bricks over. I'd almost convinced him until Gareth came screaming round the corner, 'Watch this, Tim!', and threw a brick through a window straight in front of us. Maybe that billycart to the head had really done him some damage.

STU

FF

Rosso vs technology

I read the other day that Apple has overtaken Microsoft as the most valued technology company in the world. Experts now say that consumer tastes rather than the needs of business are driving the shape of new technology.

I'll have two glasses of no shit Sherlock, please, because I'm no Bill Gates but I will tell you that no-one has ever used Excel to watch porn.

Our first computer at home was a Sinclair ZX 81, which plugged into our TV and used a tape deck to store data. This computer had 1KB of memory. Now I really should find one of those great comparisons like 'a microwave today has more computing power than the Apollo that landed on the moon' or 'your average dildo has a processor that is ten times faster than the one in the Voyager Space Shuttle' but I can't, so I'll just say that it had the tiniest memory of any computer ever on the market.

The best games in those days were still arcade games, and while all those retro cocksnaps on the internet always go on about how cool Pacman was, I still think the most underrated game was Hyper Olympics, where you would manipulate your athlete through track and field events by tapping on the control buttons as fast as you could. What I always thought was great was the discovery by bogans that you could go faster by rubbing your lighter on the buttons; down at our local pinnie parlour in Frankston you'd see some of our nation's finest in a pair of tight Faberge jeans and an East Coast windcheater proving that the Dole + Time = Invention.

If you wanted to play a game that was similar to Space Invaders on our ZX81 you had to write the program yourself using BASIC, a computer language that we were taught at school and never used again. It involved using a series of lines that started with 10 and went up to 20, 30, etc., and the computer would read each line sequentially and then act on each instruction.

This was the simplest and most juvenile program you could write.

```
10 PRINT 'DARREN LICKS HIS OWN BALLS'
20 GOTO 10
```

Mum had a Kingswood

You would then press enter and the following
would turn up on the screen.

DARREN LICKS HIS OWN BALLS
DARREN LICKS HIS OWN BALLS
DARREN LICKS HIS OWN BALLS
DARREN LICKS HIS OWN BALLS
DARREN LICKS HIS OWN BALLS
DARREN LICKS HIS OWN BALLS
DARREN LICKS HIS OWN BALLS
DARREN LICKS HIS OWN BALLS
DARREN LICKS HIS OWN BALLS
DARREN LICKS HIS OWN BALLS
DARREN LICKS HIS OWN BALLS
DARREN LICKS HIS OWN BALLS
DARREN LICKS HIS OWN BALLS
DARREN LICKS HIS OWN BALLS
DARREN LICKS HIS OWN BALLS
DARREN LICKS HIS OWN BALLS
DARREN LICKS HIS OWN BALLS
DARREN LICKS HIS OWN BALLS
DARREN LICKS HIS OWN BALLS
DARREN LICKS HIS OWN BALLS
DARREN LICKS HIS OWN BALLS
DARREN LICKS HIS OWN BALLS
DARREN LICKS HIS OWN BALLS
DARREN LICKS HIS OWN BALLS

The sad thing is that in 1985 this made for some
A-grade Year 9 entertainment.

If you wanted to get really tricky you could create a program to get your brother bad.

```
10 INPUT 'WHAT IS YOUR NAME?', A$
20 PRINT 'HELLO', A$
30 PRINT 'YOU ARE GAY'
```

Then you'd call your brother over and ask him to do the quiz, which looked like this on the screen.

WHAT IS YOUR NAME?

And he'd type in the answer and then predictably the following would flash up.

HELLO CAMPBELL YOU ARE GAY

Seriously, I'm amazed I didn't end up inventing the Hubble telescope.

It was surprising that we had this little computer before most people we knew did. The Ross family wasn't exactly known for being early adopters. It wasn't until 1981, five years after its introduction, that we finally got a colour TV. We'd spent a year changing channels with a pair of pliers on the old black and white Kreisler until the folks finally relented and got a new one. Mum and Dad didn't care about the pliers because they only ever watched the ABC. It was another eight years until we got a VCR. I think this is why I find it amazing that people put TVs that work out for council clean-up. How could you throw out something that we waited for impatiently for five years?

I used to have a mid '70s model Rank Arena TV that a friend gave me when I was living in a share house in North Melbourne. Her family got it back in the day and it must have been top of the range, with its wooden cabinet and crystal clear picture. But she assured me that it was on its last legs when I took it off her hands.

I had that TV for ten years and it was a ripper. We should have called it Beyoncé it was such a survivor. It proved to be a hero every year on Grand Final day because it was, despite its age, one of the biggest tellies around. Its specialty was outdoor screenings when Bulldog would place it on a wooden box and then hammer a tarp with a nail directly into its wooden cabinet. It finally gave up the ghost in 2004 and I almost cried; I should have given it a burial but it would have needed too big a hole.

Last year I went shopping for a combined TV/DVD player, which I know won't last for more than two years. I took Bulldog along and he quickly decided that he was the man who could do the deal because his last workplace spent fifteen grand on running a negotiating course. Of course this meant he was in the box seat to score me a bargain.

Given that I knew this item would have a limited lifespan, I set myself some simple guidelines: it had to be cheap and it had to be a brand name that not even its manufacturers had heard of, like Sonypalytronic or Sanywanky. The more obscure, the happier I'd be. I settled on a nifty unit that was priced at $319.

'Leave this one to me, mate,' said Bulldog as the pimply faced salesman came towards us.

'What's the best price you can do on this one, son?' It seemed that Bulldog had the kid on the ropes with this opening gambit.

'It's already on sale, sir, so $319 is our best offer.'

'Well, I think you can do better so why don't you go and ask your manager if he can cut us a deal or we'll go next door?'

Unfortunately for Bulldog, next door was actually a rug shop and we were in the only electronics shop in the complex, but the young chap still waddled off to see his supervisor.

Three minutes later he returned. 'I can do it for $312.'

'Done!' said Bulldog, securing a $7 discount on a no name TV/DVD.

Wow, he must have really learnt something at that negotiation course.

He was so impressed with himself that he forgot to validate the free parking, which then cost us 10 bucks, so in the end I was actually three dollars worse off.

I got my revenge on Bulldog when I series-link recorded a whole year of the children's show *Hi-5* on his Foxtel. Poor bastard; he couldn't work out why he didn't have enough memory to record the US Masters.

If Apple is proof that consumer taste is driving the computer industry, here are some products I'd like them to make.

iMower

How many times have you wished that your mower had an in-built video camera? Imagine being able to play back the vision of your neighbour using it incorrectly when they borrow it or reliving the magic of it accidentally running over your foot.

iBanana

Think of the jokes: 'What's that?' 'It's an Apple!' 'No, it's not. I think you'll find it's a banana.' Genius.

iFriend

A robotic version of Steve Jobs, who you can rely on when push comes to shove. 'Can I borrow fifty bucks, Steve?' The answer is always 'Yes' because he's loaded.

iBack

If you think the iPad or the Kindle is the future of books and magazines, think again. The iBack is a way of viewing content straight off somebody's back. You're standing on the train? Read the newspaper on someone. Are you a massage therapist who likes to read? Well then, why not read a novel while those magic hands are at work? Applying sunscreen to your partner on holiday? You can do that and check your email at the same time.

iToaster

A device that stores photos of your favourite bread, plays Jet's 'Are You Gonna Be My Girl' but still can't cook a crumpet properly? Yes, please.

iAPP

An application that can show you how to make an application that can make you a million dollars.

iShoe

Instead of laces, these futuristic shoes have a jog shuttle to do them up. They will also come with a video that explains the final series of *Lost*.

iMovie Star

Imagine being able to insert *your* head on Bruce Willis's in the *Die Hard* films? Okay, not really for everyone. Perhaps you always wanted to be the English patient in *The English Patient*? Well, this device uploads vision of your noggin and inserts you into every scene in your favourite TV show or movie. The perfect gift for mums and dads who always wanted to be Mel and Kochie.

iCAR

An electric car which has a battery that fails and can't be replaced easily, but somehow you still love it because it's cute. Where do I sign?

Nigerian loan scam

Over the last ten or so years dozens of Australians have fallen victim to Nigerian loan scams. The way these scams work is you receive a letter, email or fax from someone pretending to be in banking or from the Nigerian government and asking for your help to move large amounts of money out of the country. Of course, they explain, there's nothing illegal about this money; it often belongs to a foreigner who deposited money just before he died in a plane crash, or is the ill-gotten gains of a deposed dictator or, my personal favourite, a wealthy terminally ill person with no relatives. Naturally, the Nigerian in question is not authorised to transfer this money so they need your help. They're willing to pay you a large percentage, which is often millions of dollars, if you will assist. Once you supply them with your bank account details they ask for an advance to help bribe an official or to set up another account. Before you know it, you are handing over thousands of dollars to the scam. The worst thing is that even when people realise they are being scammed, they often hand over even more money thinking that it will all work out in the end.

I've watched these stories on *Sixty Minutes* and joined the cry, 'Why isn't the government doing anything?' Well, they never do anything. So I've come up with a solution to beat them at their own game. We don't beat New Zealand at rugby by playing them at badminton, do we? So I've knocked up an Aussie version of the scam to send their way.

Letter to a Nigerian warlord

Dear General Namibyboo

Hello, mate. I was wondering whether you could help me out with something. My brother Jason, who is a builder on the Central Coast (mostly does renos but works on a few new houses too), has just won a shitload of cash on Powerball; in fact, almost a million bucks. I'm not sure whether you have ads for Lotto in Nigeria, but if you do have ads like ours, apparently they don't actually turn up at your house with a semi-trailer full of cash—they direct debit it straight into your bank account.

Now this is where I need you to do us a favour, and it would mean heaps to my family. Jas is married to Tina, whom he met on Fairstar the Funship, one of those cruises you go on to get laid. He'd originally had a crack at her mate but she went off with a footy player from Geelong. So he hooked up with Tina and got married six months later when they thought she was preggers. It turned out that it was a false alarm but they'd paid a deposit on the venue so they thought, 'Fuck it, let's get married anyway, eh!'

They had been going pretty well until Tina decided to have it off with a couple of blokes Jas plays footy with. Jas was pretty devastated about this, even though he's no cleanskin himself. You should have seen him in action with the cougars on the dance floor in Port Douglas when we went on a golfing weekend. Crikey, the one he was with, there's no way you could have told that she was fifty!

Anyway, he wants to leave Tina and move to Bali and he doesn't want Tina to get any cash from the Powerball win. He knows she's going to take him for half the house even though the lazy bitch only worked part-time at Head Jobs hairdressing salon in Gosford.

So, mate, we need someone we can trust to help us move the cash offshore and into Indo, so the moll can't get her hands on the readies. If you're up for it we'll give you 20 per cent commission, almost 200K for helping us get the coin out.

If you're up for being a legend and helping out a bloke who's going to be financially fucked-over without your help, give us your bank account details so we can transfer the money over and then you can whack it into the account we've set up at the Bank of Kuta. Of course, you get to take your commission straightaway for being a top bloke.

Straight off the bat we've got to let you know that we're legit and we're trustworthy and you're our only hope.

But we must act fast on this, mate, because if Tina finds out about the Powerball win, nobody will get the cash and that will be a tragedy. Okay, sport?

Looking forward to getting your account details asap.

Good on you, mate.

Take care,

Stu

PART

4
Rock with Jesus, the one that pleases

When you grow up in a church-going family you do some weird shit. You don't realise it at the time; it's only in retrospect. I was having lunch recently with a mate I've known for six years and it was only then that I found out how religious his folks were and how he'd grown up without a TV. I then spent the next half hour teasing him for missing out on *The A-Team* and

Diff'rent Strokes and then I told him how we'd gone to church as kids too.

Most Sundays we'd head off to the Uniting Church in Frankston and halfway through the service we'd disappear off to Sunday School, to avoid having to listen to the sermon. We were pretty heavily involved and attended most of the children's and family camps that they put on.

One year we went away to a small country town for a family camp and we stayed in bunk beds in a room with about six other families. I would have been seven at the time, and after a couple days of art and crafts, some sloppy meals and some hardcore singing and praying it was time to let the town know about Jesus.

Someone had the brilliant idea that we'd do some home-made signs and put on some colourful costumes and march through the main street. Because it was the start of Spring, this was to be the theme and we were asked in advance to bring costumes. At the time I didn't think there was anything remotely strange about a whole bunch of people dressed in colourful clothes holding signs that said 'Jesus loves you', 'Spring is Jesus' and '*Star Wars* is the work of Satan'. Okay, I might have made the last one up.

It may have even been a little over the top for Mum, who came up with the brilliant plan to dress the family as a caterpillar. She'd taken the green conical plastic lightshade from my bedroom to make the head, and then we used a green doona to cover us to make the body. So, thankfully, as we made our way down the Main Street, we were completely hidden from view as the bemused locals came out of the pub to watch the whackos give them a well-deserved taste of the power of the Lord. After copping a barrage of abuse from young guys sitting on their utes, the parade was over and I'm pretty sure we never went on a family camp again.

As a teenager, the church did have its upside when it came to Tuesday night youth group. These gatherings were pretty low on the Bible study and tended to be nights where we'd go to the movies, learn how to cook carrot cake, or put on little skits in the church hall. My mates at school teased me mercilessly when they found out what I got up to on Tuesday nights—that is until I came to school with a hickey. Once they'd heard about the goings-on behind the church hall, they all wanted in.

In 1981, when I was ten years old, my parents decided that we'd all go and live in Fiji where Mum was going to work at a small mission hospital for six months. Dad took us off to get crew cuts to ready us for the trip, obviously concerned that they might not have a suitable barber in the small town we were heading to. Virtually hairless we sat in the front row of church that Sunday and were praised by the minister for doing the work of God, and then off we went, leaving the dog to be fed by our next door neighbours for the whole time we were away.

The nerves about our adventure were momentarily offset by the excitement of unlimited small cans of soft drink on the Qantas flight to Nadi. When we arrived at 8 that night, we were on the lookout for Arnold, the Australian doctor who was meeting us. Over the series of letters between the two, Mum had asked how she would recognise him. I can't recall what he said, but he should have said, 'I'll be the only Australian at the airport not wearing a Fiji Bitter singlet'. Arnold, a tall gangly grey-haired man in a Hawaiian shirt, packed us into his wonky old HiAce van and we took the one hour trip north-west through the dark, along the potholed roads as the tropical rain started to pour.

When we arrived at the mission hospital, Arnold took us straight to our new home, a small old weatherboard house, with one bedroom, a small kitchen/lounge room and a bathroom. My brothers and I were to stay in the annexed part of the padre's house that was 20 metres away from our parent's house. The enclosed verandah of this 1920s house was bare apart from the three old hospital beds. It had an outdoor bathroom with a shower with no hot water, complete with a frog that would pop out of the drain every time you turned the tap on and never failed to scare the shit out of us. This was pretty primitive stuff.

The mission compound had a small hospital, a church, a building where the nurses lived, a primary school, and an assortment of houses for doctors and staff. Dotted with mango and hibiscus trees, the lush green grass almost seemed to grow in front of your eyes, relishing the tropical heat and rain.

We went off to the local schools—Campbell and Stephen went to the Catholic high school in town, and I went to the mission primary school. My first day was extremely confronting; being the only white kid there made me feel incredibly self-conscious. My teacher Miss Mohammed was a Fijian Indian with a prosthetic arm. The story I was told by one of the boys at lunchtime was that her husband had suspected that she'd been having an affair, so had hacked off her arm with a cane knife and taken it with him when he jumped into a taxi. Or so the story went. He had taken off her right arm and she had had to learn to write with her left. Her plastic prosthetic arm had kindly been donated by an organisation in Australia so unfortunately it was white. Someone had done a very average job of painting it with brown paint to try and make it match her skin tone. It hadn't worked, small sections of it had chipped away and you could see the original colouring as she walked around the classroom with it dangling awkwardly from her sari.

The classroom was like something out of the 1950s— wooden chairs and desks, ancient schoolbooks and a discipline regime that was frightening. There were two deaf girls in the class who were dressed in their purple uniforms and sent off to school every day, but simply sat there and did nothing. Every year they went up a class with little or no effort to teach them anything. On my second day, one of them sat there harmlessly scribbling on a piece of paper. Miss Mohammed noticed this and slapped her across the head, almost knocking the poor girl to the ground. I was horrified but worse was to come. The next day one of the boys was cutting up some cardboard with his scissors when he was supposed to be writing an essay. She picked up the scissors in a rage and cut into the top part of his ear; blood spurted everywhere as he howled in pain. That was enough for me and I never went back to that school again. So for the next few months I just hung out with Dad and we'd get the little orange windowless buses into town to buy food from the markets and then head to the library to borrow more books which we were devouring at a rate of knots because Fiji had no television in those days. On one of our trips into town a big, toothless bus driver gave me an old Fijian penny that had a hole in the middle of it. Dad explained that Fijians used to carry their money on a piece of string around their neck, so I went home and got a piece of string tied it around my neck and proudly wore it the whole time we were there. It always got me a wonderful smile from any old timers who saw it.

Late one afternoon we were coming home from town as a cyclone was about to hit. The bus was full of people who'd come in to stock up on kava (the root that Fijians grind and add to water and drink as a relaxant) and grab some rope to tie down their tin homes. The bus was just leaving the small terminal when the rain and the wind hit, and everyone rushed to unroll the plastic windows and pull them down to protect us from the oncoming storm. It was useless; within minutes we were saturated. By the time we hit the single lane bridge that crossed the Ba River, the rain was coming sideways straight into the bus and the river was quickly rising. I looked at the old man who was doing an unconvincing job of putting on a brave face as we slowly chugged across the bridge in almost zero visibility.

As we neared the end I looked out of the window and saw that the river had reached the top of the bridge and was continuing to rise at an alarming rate. It looked like we could get swept away as the howling wind continued to knock the bus around. The sound of Indian pop songs could still be faintly heard crackling through the bus's tinny speakers as the river rose and all that could be seen was the top half of the railing just as we reached the last 5 metres of the bridge. And then we were safely across. When we looked back we could no longer see the bridge at all.

The bus crawled its way to the hospital where we jumped out and clambered into the house. Mum and my brothers were waiting for us. Then the wind really picked up. Palm branches hit the side of the house and the roar of thunder accompanied the sheet lightning that lit up the sky. There was nothing to do other than wait and hope the little house would hold together until the cyclone passed. We heard a strange noise outside and peeked out the small window to see what was going on. As the next round of lightning struck we saw a white horse on its hind legs, completely petrified, it's squealing whinnies piercing through the cacophony of the storm. Thankfully, we were through the worst of it and only the solid rain continued. In the morning, the compound was a mess with uprooted trees covering roads and debris everywhere but we'd got through the worst of the two cyclones that we would experience in our time there.

I'd spend a bit of time kicking around the hospital, particularly the children's ward where I'd become friends with a Fijian boy called Aquila. He was a funny little kid with the widest smile you'd ever seen. He'd bravely pushed his little sister out of the way of an oncoming truck only to have it run over his foot. It was rather badly mangled and after initial treatment it was decided he needed skin grafts. On the morning of his operation he asked me to hand him the biscuits that were on the nurse's desk. I grabbed them for him, he ate three or four of them hungrily, and then motioned to me to put them back. When the nurse came back she looked at me and told me not to give Aquila any biscuits because he wasn't allowed to eat before his operation. I asked her why and she said that it was dangerous to have food in your stomach if you were having a general anaesthetic. I was panicking; Aquila's English was patchy so he hadn't understood what was going on. I was too scared to let the nurse know that I had actually given him the biscuits. On the other hand I wasn't exactly keen to have my little mate die on the operating table. Sitting there as another nurse came into to prep him, I raced out of the children's ward to find Mum and tell her the truth. She was in the women's ward and I told her the whole story. Instead of reprimanding me, Mum thanked me for telling her and they simply rescheduled the surgery and there was no harm done.

After the surgery Aquila cried a lot not just from the pain but because he was like any seven-year-old kid away from his parents for months. He had a scar the size of a small tissue box where the skin graft was taken from his leg. When it healed I found it bizarre that he had a rectangular patch of white skin slap bang on his black leg.

One afternoon his whole family turned up to see him, and when I say 'whole' I mean his *whole* family. Cousins, aunts, uncles, at least thirty of them in total, and unfortunately they wouldn't let them all into the cramped children's ward to see him. This was upsetting for the family who'd made an enormous effort to get there, and Aquila was naturally disappointed too. There was nothing else to be done so I commandeered a wheelchair, put him in it and took the lot of them up to our house (we had moved from the smaller place to a bigger, more comfortable house) where they could all talk to each other. It was amazing to have this wonderful smiling, laughing family completely filling up our lounge room as Dad happily made cups of tea for everyone. Aquila was ecstatic.

Mum was working long hours at the understaffed hospital and would often come home with blood splattered all over her feet and sandals. Dad would walk Mum down to the hospital at night and on more than one occasion when the power failed found himself holding a Dolphin torch while Mum brought the latest Fijian into the world. At other times the security guard Akbal, a Fijian Indian who carried a star picket, would walk Mum safely home.

He invited us to his home in the hills for lunch one day and we took the bus up to his house, which was little more than a concrete slab with two rooms with corrugated iron walls and a roof. In this modest structure he lived with his wife and three children. A poor but generous man, he had slaughtered his only goat to make us lunch that day, and the five us sat at a rickety wooden table and ate the curry with Roti and rice while the whole family watched, as is their tradition. It was an extremely humbling feeling to know that they were happy to have us eat before them, especially knowing how significant the animal was to them. He didn't have much, but he was prepared to share it all with us as his way of thanking Mum for the contribution she was making to the health of his community.

During our stay, three travelling young Christians arrived, a girl from Australia, another from New Zealand, and a bloke from America called Frank. These evangelists were so full-on that the old man quickly dubbed the Yank 'Fundamentalist Frank'.

They held classes in the church where they gave out packs of chewing gum for challenges like finding a certain passage in the Bible first. We happily went along, drawn in by the chewie. In the afternoon Frank took everyone aside for five minutes. Sitting in a small sparse room off the main section of the blue-painted rendered-concrete church he sat me down and asked me whether I was prepared to give up my life for Jesus Christ. I never realised that it was God's plan for some fuckwit American to set the timetable for when I decided to make a solid decision about faith, but I found the entire experience incredibly intimidating. He kept leaning in and asking me over and over again 'Will you, Tim, give up your life for Jesus?' At ten years of age it was impossible for me to fathom or judge. Entirely confused, I told him I wasn't sure and left. I was completely disturbed by the situation and asked Campbell how he'd felt. He looked at me, nonplussed, and said, 'I just said yes and took the chewie!' Up until that point I had spent a lot of time around the church, with wonderful, kind people, and this was the first time I had felt uneasy, and Frank's question is one that I still can't answer to this day.

Aquila was discharged not long before we left to go home to Australia and despite sending him a few letters over the next few years I never heard from him again.

5
The electrifying '80s

You only have to visit Old Parliament House in Canberra to realise how dinky Australia was in the 1980s. If you wander into the prime minister's office you realise that it was right at the front of the building, only a couple of storeys up with windows facing the street. Back in the day you could have driven past and yelled out 'Bob Hawke's a cunt' and he probably would have heard you.

It was during this time that Australia won the America's Cup and I had my first spew from alcohol. Not much was going right for old Oz then; we'd just had a terrible drought, the economy was stuffed, so we clung on to a yacht race that no-one else in the world including the Americans gave a rat's arse about.

So in 1983 I headed off to a party with my brothers wearing a 'We've won it' America's Cup T-shirt that my uncle gave me and decided to drink half a bottle of mandarin liqueur with lemonade. I was having a right old time running around abusing people and was certainly worse for wear when Mum picked us up at the crazy time of 9.30. I certainly picked a bad night to experiment with alcohol because Nanna was in the front seat of the Commodore when I projectile vomited all over the back seat and our friend Carolyn's leg (Mum had kindly offered her a lift home). I don't think anyone was buying my 'Someone must have spiked the punch' line and it was sad to see Nanna inspecting my handiwork as Mum scrubbed the carpet and I made my way to bed. The car smelt of spew for weeks and, needless to say, to this day I can't drink mandarin liqueur. Not that I have ever come across a bottle of it since.

From then on Mum was pretty strict with me, so a few years later I took to sneaking out to go to parties if she wouldn't let me go. One night I did my normal trick of lumping some clothes and my stackhat under the doona to give the impression that I was in bed asleep and climbed out my window and headed off to the party on my bike. Returning a little wobbly after knocking over a $3.99 cask of Fruity Lexia with my mates, I climbed in through my window to find my that my old teddy bear had been placed in the bed and was snuggling up next to my stackhat. I'd been so busted. When I got up in the morning Mum didn't say anything to me. It was her way of letting me know that she knew what I'd been up to. She was always inventive in the way that she dealt with us and I presume it gave her a kick. During the school holidays when we'd proved to be a bit shabby with doing our chores while she was at work, she took the TV cable that ran from the TV to the antenna socket with her to work so we couldn't watch the box. Her cunning plan backfired though because instead of getting outside and cleaning up the garden, I spent the whole day trying to fashion coaxial cable out of electrical wire, a coat hanger and gaffer tape. Not that it worked.

Bikes were still our major mode of transport and gave us a sense of independence, especially during school holidays. In the days before mobile phones, we'd just get on our bikes and turn up at our mate's house, then they'd grab their bike and we'd cycle on to the next destination. One day we decided to head down to see our mate Troy, who lived on a small farm in Hastings, which was at least 25 kilometres away. After spending the best part of two hours getting there, we knocked on the door only to find that he wasn't home, so we simply turned round and cycled home again.

My girlfriend was certainly home when I went round to see her during the holidays. With her mum at work and her dad away, we magically found ourselves doing some awkward teenage touching. The romance was halted when from her second-storey bedroom window I saw her dad's ute turn into the driveway. Unsurprisingly, panic set in. I was in bed with his daughter and he was a rather large and scary Italian concreter who just happened to have a shotgun in his car, fresh from a duck-hunting trip with his mates. Now this bloke almost took my head off for leaving the lid off the Milo the last time I was around there, so who knew what he was capable of if he saw my superfade stretch Edwin jeans lying on his little princess's bedroom floor.

Terrified, I grabbed my clothes and hid in her cupboard where I stayed for the next five hours until the family headed out to a friend's place for dinner. I was still shaking as I rode my bike home in the dark.

I'm not sure whether people have rumpus rooms anymore, but in the 1970s they were massive. They tended to be rooms that contained a ping-pong table, another TV or a billiard table and were places where kids could go mad and not give their parents the shits.

Ours was a little on the low-rent side and housed Mum's sewing machine, the ironing board and an upright piano that none of us ever learnt how to play. I did put the rumpus room to good use one day after school with another girlfriend when we chose it as a new location to have a special cuddle. It was a hot February day and among the throes of what could barely be described as passion I looked out the window only to spot the old man wandering around watering the garden in his undies. Petrified we hit the deck; thankfully he hadn't seen us.

There's a strange moment in your adolescence when your relationship with your parents changes. It came to be summed up for me as the change from the excitement of yelling 'Yay, Daddy's home!' to the sheer dread of 'Fuck, the old man's home!' When the slightest glance of us lying on the couch watching *The Goodies* could set the old man right off. Tired and hungry after a shit day at work was there a worse time for him to find out I'd spilt orange cordial on the carpet ... again? Not that the living room carpet was sacred—it had a multitude of alternative uses, the best being a convenient abrasive for the dog to rub his arse on with the theme to *Perfect Match* as his soundtrack.

I found fewer things more embarrassing than going shopping for clothes with Mum. Teenage boys are hilarious when they try and pretend they're not actually with their mum in a shoe store.

The worst thing happened when I was in Myer at Frankston getting a new pair of jeans one day after school. I was pretty keen on a new pair of Levis when I spied a few girls that I knew. As they came closer, Mum announced rather loudly, 'It's no good, you're too little for these jeans. We'll have to go to the boys section.' Giggling the girls followed us over and watched and laughed as Mum checked out whether the jeans fit me by putting her hand down the back of my jeans. The girls didn't need Facebook to get that story around.

Luckily Mum didn't come with me when I got a haircut. Most of the time we'd get our hair cut at this strange little place called Just for Men. A gay guy called Frank ran it, keeping the lads happy about his sexuality by employing ample-breasted women. At fourteen you could sit there in your school uniform, smoking a cigarette, drinking a cup of Nescafé and get a trim for 15 bucks. The big attraction was that you didn't need an appointment and it was cheap. One afternoon after school, my mate Bulldog and I found ourselves in there at the same time. I lucked out and got Tracy in the tight Faberge jeans and the stilettos while poor old Bulldog got Frank. Frank was loud and flamboyant; on sitting Bulldog down, he looked at his forehead and camply declared, 'Oh my god, look at the size of that pimple!' and proceeded to bop it with his comb at which it exploded everywhere.

I hit '80s fashion pretty hard and in 1985 I decided I needed a special outfit to attend the Spandau Ballet concert at the entertainment centre. Sitting on a hanger on Mum's door was a black jacket with padded shoulders which looked pretty similar to the ones that all the pop stars were wearing in *Smash Hits* magazine. I tried it on with a white shirt and a cowboy tie, and I thought I was styling! We caught the train to the city and had a great time at the gig, which as you'd expect was full of teenage girls. One particular girl from our area caught my eye and we ended up sitting together on the train home. She loved my jacket, which I told her I'd bought at a trendy men's boutique in South Yarra.

She was cute and funny and we had a shared taste in shit bands so it was all going on. When we got to Frankston we walked towards the phone booth to ring our respective parents to get them to pick us up. Trying to be ever so cool I offered her a Peter Jackson light blue cigarette which she took and as we puffed, I decided it was time to go in for the pash. Just as our lips were about to meet a car stopped in front of us and I heard Mum's voice: 'Timothy, what are you doing smoking and what the hell are you doing wearing my new jacket?'

She'd been out to dinner and had decided to just come to the station and wait for me.

The magic disappeared as my new crush looked at my embarrassed face and as I sheepishly removed Mum's jacket and got in the car. I don't think I ever saw the girl again.

My next girlfriend had an enormous split-level house with an intercom system connected throughout. Something must have snapped in people's heads back then because suddenly just yelling from one end of the house to the other was passé and what everyone needed was a two-way system so you could chat to your kids when they were barely two rooms away. While my girlfriend was out in the lounge room doing some homework I was mucking around pushing buttons on the intercom.

Suddenly I heard an Uh, Uh, Uh, Uh noise and I couldn't work out what was going on until I heard her dad's voice say, 'Did you come, Julie?'. Shuddering I realised I'd been eavesdropping on her parent's Saturday afternoon sex. It was rather disturbing.

6
The power of apricot jam

My dear old mum Jennifer did an amazing job balancing a career and having a family. In the late 1960s when my eldest brother Stephen was a baby, as she was hanging nappies out on the clothes line, she said to herself, 'There's got to be more to life than this', and promptly went back to work at the Fairfield Hospital one day a week. Throughout the 1970s she worked part-time.

In the early 1980s Mum opened up her own surgery and I'd spend a lot of time there after school. When

I wasn't eating the jellybeans meant for the kids after they'd had an injection, Mum had me doing chores. Two of my jobs seemed equally gross—it's impossible to work out which was the worst. My indoor job was to clean the speculums, the metal devices that doctors used for Pap smears. I had to scrub them with a toothbrush and then pop them in the steriliser.

The outside job was the disposal of medical waste. This was the '80s, so incinerators were at their peak. If it was flammable, burn it, was the motto back then—and even if it wasn't, you'd still give it a go. That structure out the back made of breezeblocks was a convenient substitute for the yet-to-be-invented council clean-up and the suburbs were awash with plumes of black smoke as dads everywhere tried to answer one of life's trickier questions: Can you burn a beanbag? Yes you can, with the help of a little bit of petrol. Anyway, after school I'd take a plastic Safeway bag full of manky dressings, bandages and needles and set fire to them, then sit back and enjoy the fumes. Without exception a piece of pus-soaked gauze would land on my black Harrison school shoes and I'd have to pick it up with a stick and wipe any infectious residue off on the grass.

Being one of the few female doctors in the area at that

time, Mum was very popular with women and many teenage girls from my brother's school would go and see her. This became a big problem for Stephen because of the photo Mum had of us on her desk. Like a scene out of *Puberty Blues*, they'd be asking about going on the Pill and then burst out laughing when they saw the bowl haircuts we had in the photo.

I knew that Mum was always having to get up in the middle of the night to deliver babies, but I never thought much about how often she saw death or how the death of her patients might affect her. When we were kids, Mum found an elderly lady, Mrs Evans, to babysit us and do some ironing. She was fabulous with us and she and her husband became like grandparents. When I was a teenager and my brothers had moved out of home, it was great when she was there on Monday afternoons doing the ironing. I'd sit and talk to her about sport and she'd always come and see me in school plays. She was positive, upbeat and a lovely woman. When she became extremely sick and had to go into hospital, it was the first time I saw Mum really concerned. The specialists looked at Mrs Evans and put her on a series of drugs but she was going downhill fast. In a last-ditch attempt to save her life Mum took her off all the medication and to everyone's surprise she came good and she lived for another ten years.

Mum has always loved dogs so they were our childhood pets. Ted was our first dog and he was a cheeky little bugger. A classic bitzer, he was always getting into trouble. When our neighbours' dog was on heat they would lock her under the house to keep the local boy dogs away from her. Every morning they'd take her out for a walk and then put her back in and lock the door. Ted had obviously observed this, and being pretty smart he snuck in under their house during the morning constitutional. Of course, when they returned he got locked in too. I'm sure our little mate had the time of his life. Mum and Dad took this opportunity to explain to us about the birds and the bees. I think my brothers got it, but for years I thought you had to go under the neighbours' house if you wanted a baby.

Ted's luck ran out when he was hit by a car, and we didn't have another dog for years until Mum came home with a little white puppy that had wandered in alone into her surgery that afternoon. It was supposed to go to the lost dog's home the next day but of course it stayed. Chloe, like Ted, used to love to roam the neighbourhood and was everyone's friend. It cost Mum a fortune in fines from the council because whenever the dog catcher came around, Chloe would run up to them tail wagging and jump straight into their waiting arms. Fifteen years later, when old age had made her life so hard she had to be put down, the vet was kind enough to come round to Mum's house to do it, so Chloe's buried in the backyard with a tree growing over her.

Mum's a whiz in the kitchen and I'll always be grateful that she took the time to teach me how to cook. I loved cooking so much as a kid that my brothers nicknamed me Margaret Fulton. Experimentation was my thing and when we got the microwave oven I was out to prove that anything could be cooked in it. One time I made a damper-like batter from flour and water and added a couple of teaspoons of strawberry Quik to make what I ingeniously called 'strawberry scones'.

After microwaving them on high for three minutes, I took them out. These pink mounds were rock hard and unsurprisingly tasted like shit. Angry at my culinary disaster, I went out on to the balcony and threw them into the bush next door. Months later I was walking home up the path and I spied one in the grass looking exactly the same as it had when it came out of the oven. Not even the feral animals would eat it.

One of Mum's great triumphs was her apricot jam. Nanna and Poppa had an extremely productive apricot tree that bore enormous amounts of fruit, so every year mum would make a big batch of jam. I have never met a person who has not lost their mind over Mum's jam and to this day I still grab a jar every time I go and see her.

When I was nineteen, I went to Byron Bay with some mates and rented a flat opposite Clarke's beach. There was a bunch of extremely attractive girls from Sydney in the flat next door and we quickly became friends. Naturally, I'd brought up a jar of the jam and somehow one of the girls had tasted it, so that every morning they'd all stream into our flat, carrying toast on their plates and wearing little more than a T-shirt and their undies, to hook into Mum's apricot jam. I remember silently thanking Mum every time: 'Oh dear Mum, I love you so.' It was a very good holiday.

MORE STUFF

→

STU

FF

Relationships

Most sex therapists (when they're not masturbating feverishly) will tell you that variety is the key to maintaining a healthy and rewarding sex life especially when you've been with someone for so long that you don't even blink an eyelid when they drop their guts while putting on a pair of tracky pants. Dress-ups and role-playing can form a key part in keeping things fresh—but some of these traditional fantasies have become a little old hat. Time to say 'Goodbye' to the naughty nurse, the bad schoolgirl, the horny fireman, and the fat-cat suit, and say 'Hello' to these saucy characters that are guaranteed to get the most out of your Viagra prescription.

The Game Show Host

Since the early days of television, game shows have been the closest thing we've had to fully fledged pornography. People winning shit is hot! To engage in this fantasy, the man in the relationship will need to make a Larry Emdur mask from a scanned photo of him on the bourbon and cokes at a friend's bucks' night. If you weren't at that particular event, you could easily do a Google image search. Once the mask is on, chant 'Come on down' until the love-making reaches its climax.

The Sleazy Guy at Work

What woman hasn't fantasised over the revolting guy at work who thinks he's a stud? Why risk an HR disaster when your man can offer to give you a massage while you work at your laptop at the kitchen table. This succeeds best with well thought out, sexy dialogue like, 'Wow, Veronica, you look tense. You need old magic hands to weave some of his, um, magic.' 'Fuck off, Graham, you sleazebag.' Hot.

The Fireman (on a Disability Pension)

Girls, take this class fantasy one step further by dressing your man up in a fireman's uniform, then making him sit in a wheelchair. Dance seductively for him to an obscure Evermore album track, and wait for him to sob, 'It's no good, I still can't feel my legs!'

The Passive-Aggressive Bitch in Your Netball Team

Take lovemaking into the cyber world as you email antagonistic emails under the guise of that bitch from your netball team. He won't be able to control himself as he opens up emails about mistakes in the fixture and who owes whom for petrol money. Sexy.

The Unhelpful Customs Guy

Do you remember that time you just got off the plane from Bali, the kids were screaming, your head was thumping because your braids were tied too tight, and then some numb nuts in a blue shirt gave you the third degree over an undeclared wood carving that you didn't want to buy in the first place. Somewhere in the back of your mind you may have found this hot. Dress your man up and show him exactly what you want to declare ... that you're horny. Cavity search anyone?

Foxtel Installer

You're looking for a world of entertainment? Well this role-play will take tantric sex to the next level when your lover guarantees to come somewhere between noon and 4pm.

The Domestic Qantas Hostie

As you get older and not everything is where you would like it to be, you have to adjust your role-playing to suit. Put your hubby in the Jason recliner, fill an old pram with bottles of Jacobs Creek and roll on past him. When he attempts to stop you, snarl at him, 'Sorry, darl, you've had too much to drink!' Sexy.

Matt Preston

Similarly, for the gents, if you're not exactly at your ideal playing weight, adopt a plummy accent, tie a cravat around your woo woo, and declare, 'Anyone for a taste test?' Bon Appetite!

The Taxi Driver

For this wonderful scenario you'll need a late-model Ford Falcon, a blue shirt, a pair of gardening gloves, and the radio tuned to Mix-FM or any similar easy-listening station. The rest is up to your imagination. Hint: deodorant is very much optional.

The Undertaker

Dressed in a dark-coloured suit with his hair slicked to the side with Brylcreem, your man stands with his hands together in front of him, and solemnly intones, 'I'm sorry for your loss, would you like a root?' This scenario works best when the woman says, 'Yes'.

Party games

I've always staunchly believed that games nights are for nerds or for people who are so competitive that it makes them borderline psychopathic. You know the type, they invite you round for dinner and straight after they whip out the Trivial Pursuit board quicker than you can say, 'I would never have believed anyone could fuck up a Bill Granger recipe so royally, but you did', and then take it all so seriously you would swear that you were in Churchill's War Cabinet room.

The problem with games is they haven't updated with the times, so here's my take on a few old favourites.

Twister reloaded
Twister was invented back in the '60s as an excuse for people to touch each other because 'doing it' was still frowned on a bit. The first edition had five rows of circles—green, yellow,

blue, red and brown—but the latter was dropped after some confusion occurred when people were given the instruction 'Right hand brown'.

But in this age of internet porn, online dating and snuggies, people don't need some silly pretence to rub themselves up against someone they're attracted to.

So, to take it to the next level, invite some friends over and surprise them by taking them to the mid-West of America where you wait around for a real Twister to come. When you are all sucked in by the tornado, whoever survives when they are thrown into a farmer's barn at 150 kilometres per hour is the winner.

Alicia Keyes party

Key parties were a massive phenomenon in the 1970s. On arrival, all the men would chuck their keys into a bowl. The guests would party on normally and at the end of the night the ladies would pick a random key out of the bowl and go home with the dude who owned it.

This version is the same as the original but after the key is selected and the two head off for good times, the man has to sing 'Falling' by Alicia Keyes while making love.

Daihatsu charades

For an automotive twist on this party classic, take a Daihatsu Charade down to the local oval and carve out the required imagery on grass by doing burn outs. Circle work has never been this cerebral.

Extreme paper rock scissors

One of life's questions I've always pondered is how come if people are supposed to be our friends, why do they give us the shits so much? Well, why not excommunicate yourself from your group with 'paper rock scissors'? This is an awesome way to let the Carpenters know that they won't be going to Bali with the rest of you.

Office limbo

Just like a normal game of limbo with a broom stick, but at the end of the game when one super-flexible person is feeling pretty pleased with themselves your boss comes out and announces that your company is being put into liquidation and it will be weeks until anyone knows who will keep their jobs.

Duopoly

Monopoly is fun but collusion means you get to share the joys of winning as you engage in some old-fashioned illegal price-fixing to put a small business into receivership. Can be played concurrently with office limbo.

Adult Connect Four
See Alicia Keyes party.

Industry Scrabble
We all know there's nothing worse than someone who talks about his or her job all the time—or is there? Nothing will get people looking at their watches quicker than a game of industry Scrabble where all the words laid on the board have to relate to your chosen field. Dr Wilson has just put 'colonoscopy' on a triple word score! Brian the investment banker has just done 'diversify' but then all hell breaks loose when Steve from State Rail tries to argue that 'rostered day off' is one word.

Super Uno
Just like the normal game, but the first person to be super Aussie and pronounce the game 'you-no' wins Pauline Hanson's house.

PART

7
I lied about being the outdoors type

If there's one thing I've learnt in life, it's never lend a tent to a friend.

No matter who they are they will always lose a pole or leave something stinky rolled up inside. The problem is you never realise this until you are 5 kilometres deep into the bush of the Blue Mountains, with half an hour of sunlight to get your camp sorted, and a quick inventory of pegs and poles leaves the scream of, 'Fuck you, Davo!' echoing through the wilderness.

The old man was a keen Scout and Scout leader when he was younger, which would make you think that he was bang up for taking his three sons camping. Despite him having all the gear, the knot-tying prowess, enormous experience and a swag full of shit songs from the gang show, he never took us all camping. Not that I'm complaining. He did once kill a copperhead snake with a shovel after it had decided to join us in the sand pit when we were little. That was pretty tough in our book. What was even more impressive was that he preserved the snake in a jar of formaldehyde so every year for show and tell we had a ready-made Exhibit A. I can just imagine our teachers in the staffroom kicking back with a Winfield and a mug of International Roast:

'Any guesses on what Tim Ross brought in for show and tell this morning?'

'Not that fucking snake in a jar?'

'Bingo!'

'That family has been trotting that thing out for years? Anyone want a Monte Carlo biscuit?'

'No, thanks, I'm on the Richard Simmons work out

diet. Did anyone see *Dallas* last night? Who do you think shot JR?'

When Dad bought a second-hand tent from a friend that did get some excitement going. Surely owning a tent meant going camping? Not really.

We did get close when Dad decided to have a test run by erecting it in our lounge room. Obviously the pegs were an issue, but Dad got around this problem by nailing the fly ropes and the base tags to the floor with flat-headed galvanised nails. We were out of minds with excitement: we had a tent in our lounge room and we could spend the night in it. Strangely enough this dry run never turned into the real thing until Campbell took matters into his own hands and asked Dad to take him camping for his tenth birthday. Dad relented and it was a big thing to watch them pack up Dad's Suzuki 4WD with sleeping bags, the esky and the tent and watch them head off for their night away. Stephen and I were very jealous.

So we were a bit surprised to see them arrive home sheepishly a few hours later while we were watching *Minder*. It seemed that the old man had only driven about 10 kilometres up the road and picked a spot in a small piece of bush on the Seaford Foreshore, barely 20 metres from the busy Nepean Highway. They'd only just set up camp when a bloke from the council walked past and told them to pack up and move on. Dad had essentially taken Campbell camping in a local park.

Any major outdoor activity from then on was restricted to school camps, where we'd inevitably come across those weird, bearded mountain-loving types that Australia produced so well in the 1970s and early '80s. These types were sick for a kayak, wore beanies and long johns and substituted masturbating for orienteering. At night on these camps, when we were asleep and the teachers were smashing a cask of Coolabah by the fire and character-assassinating our juvenile personalities, Bearded Guy would be making a necklace of gumnuts, magpie feathers and fishing line while snacking on a bag of scroggin (a mixture of nuts, dried fruit and chocolate designed to give you energy while hiking).

On my Year 8 camp at Gippsland in Victoria, there was one of these chaps. Nicknamed 'Bullant' because of his deep-set eyes, this guy would have lived off bark alone if he could have. Wiry from years of kayaking and digging shallow graves, he showed a sadistic love of twisting boys underwater in their kayaks so we could get the hang of releasing the waterproof skin that kept the water out of the vessel and pulling ourselves out and making our way to the surface. After seeing three of my mates suffer through this torture, I elected to take the safer option of canoeing down the river.

If Bullant had been on *Man vs Wild* with Bear Grylls, on the first sign of starvation he would have stabbed Grylls in the head with a branch, eaten his flesh raw and worn his skin as a Parka.

On the final day of camp, happy to be heading home, we piled on the bus and said, 'G'day', to Bill the Bus Driver. He was a friendly bloke in his mid forties who always had a beaming smile. It was only years later that we found out the secret to his eternal happiness—his specialty was seducing the lonely mums who went on school excursions and camps. The dirty old bugger.

As we headed down the long gravel driveway, at the urging of my mates I leant out the window and screamed: 'See you later, Bullant, you fuckwit!' We all laughed, even Bill the Casanova Bus Driver cracked a smile.

Unfortunately, Bullant didn't find it hilarious and started running through the paddocks, yelling, 'Bill! Stop the bus!' He was a man possessed, sprinting like a Terminator until he finally caught up with the bus at the bend of the road and Bill relented and stopped. He jumped on board, grabbed me, dragged me off the bus by my collar and then threw me up against the back of the bus. Holding on to the front of my jacket, he shoved me into the bus on the beat of every word: 'Ross ... I've ... tried ... damn ... hard ... with ... you ... this ... week ...you ... are ... a ... fucking ... imbecile ...' Eventually, emotionally exhausted, he let go of me and wandered off into the bush. Still in a state of shock, I got back on the bus to a standing ovation and even Bill gave me a look of deep respect. Well, at least I think he did; then again he was probably just reminiscing about doing Adam Matthews's mum in the back of her Mercedes.

In Year 12 a couple of my mates, Jamo and Ben, were boarders and my English teacher, who was also a boarding master, offered to take them fishing for the weekend. It was a nice gesture because the lads' parents lived overseas, and I tagged along for the ride. Jamo knew a little place on a river a few hours away, so off we went, set up our tents and tried to land some fish. We soldiered on without any luck and were forced to retire to light the fire and cook some steaks. We had bought some beers and The Teacher had brought a bottle of red. Feeling just a little bit *Dead Poets Society*, we sat around the fire talking the sort of pseudo-intellectual rubbish only Year

12 students can talk with their English teacher. The next morning The Teacher was so hung-over he could barely get out of his tent. We fished for a few more hours until we really had to pack up and head home. After driving for no more than 5 kilometres, The Teacher had to pull over and have a spew. He was a tall, gangly bloke with a slight lisp—and he was the first and only person I've ever heard vomit with a slight lisping sound. With last night's dinner successfully spread out over a park bench, he crashed out near the swings in the park.

After half an hour of watching him slumped near the swings, I was starting to have doubts; we'd gone from 'O Captain, my Captain' to 'How the hell are we going to get home? The Captain has spew on his V-neck'. The Teacher finally got up and sat behind the wheel of the car before his head hit the steering wheel and he mumbled, 'It's no use, I can't drive. Can somebody else, please?' Stunned, we looked at each other, not a driver's licence between us, and then Jamo piped up, 'I'll drive!'

So with The Teacher asleep in the front seat, Jamo took us all the way home. Parking the car in The Teacher's driveway, we helped him to the door and he swore us to secrecy. After I graduated, I was chatting to another teacher from school at the pub, a rather pompous Englishman who smoked Silk Cut cigarettes, drove a Jaguar and tragically rated himself rather highly for staging a Year 10 production of *Macbeth*. I mentioned The Teacher's name and his eyes grew wide, 'He is dangerous—he masturbates young men's minds!' I'm still not sure about that but he certainly was a lightweight on the claret.

While I was at uni, I became mates with a couple of country boys, Scotty and Mud. They loved fishing and they took me up to the Snowy Mountains where we slept in swags and managed to catch absolutely nothing. Being true country larrikins, the boys had some weird ways. They were obsessed with the old 'Have you seen this?' game. This is where you'd be sitting there fishing, enjoying the quiet trickle of the stream, when one of them would suddenly say, 'Oh my God. Check this out!' and you'd turn round and they'd have their nob resting on a can of VB. Then they'd 'Got you!' for looking. It was weird but strangely amusing and they certainly enjoyed their exhibitionist ways, getting me with their 'Have you read this?' (nob in a newspaper); 'Do you reckon this will work as bait?' (nob too close to a fishing hook for comfort); and my personal favourite: 'Does anyone want a sausage roll?' (nob in sausage roll wrapper, thankfully *sans* sauce).

As impressive as their antics were, things certainly hit a peak when we went to one of their friend's farms. The parents of a schoolmate who was overseas, these hospitable country folk kindly cooked us a roast dinner. I excused myself to go to the bathroom leaving Scotty and Mud to chat to the mum in the kitchen. When I returned they both had stupid smiles on their faces, and when I got closer I realised why. Both of them were standing behind the island bench chatting away to the mum while she was making gravy, totally oblivious to their cocks hanging out of their moleskins. They had truly gone insane.

Bulldog also dragged me up to the Snowy Mountains to go to the small town of Walwa. Sitting right on the Murray in the north-east of Victoria, it has a population of 268. At the time Bulldog was a carpenter and had just finished an extension on the Walwa Bush Nursing Hospital. A few things needed to be checked on, so we decided to make a weekend of it. We jumped into his big F150 ute and chugged out up the Princes Highway. He loved this car but unfortunately he was the only person in the universe to opt for 'theft-only' on the fire and theft option on his insurance. As fate would have it, his car caught fire one day while he was driving down Punt Road. Struggling to dowse the flames with a St Kilda scarf and half a can of Tarax Wild Raspberry, he was lucky that a bloke with a fire extinguisher stopped and put it out before it exploded in front of him.

Anyway, after a few hours on the road we stopped at a servo for the full truckers' breakfast of eggs, steak, bacon, tomato and chips. I'd been off the smokes for six months and had really started to enjoy my food, and was getting the waistline to prove it. On the way out I grabbed a Picnic bar. I opened it as we moved back out onto the highway, and Bulldog looked at me and looked at the Picnic and said with disgust, 'Do you really need that?' I thought to myself, 'You'll keep!'

When we rolled into Walwa, there wasn't much to the town apart from the hospital, a general store and the pub, where we'd decided to stay for the night. It had a classic old public bar and the ice cold pots of Carlton were going down a treat as Bulldog introduced me to the mates he'd made in the six months he'd worked there. They were a motley bunch of mountain men who weren't quite sure what to make of this mid '90s indie rocker in his cords, 1970s body shirt, Converse All Star shoes and brown cardigan.

Ron the Publican, a big bloke with a beer gut that deserved its own postcode, took me through the lounge to show me our room while Bulldog stayed in the public bar, catching up with his pals.

As he opened the door to the dingy brown-carpeted room revealing two single beds, I sighed and said, 'Oh well, this will have to do, I suppose. We can just push the beds together.' On that note, Ron hightailed it back to the front bar and within a minute Bulldog came storming up the hallway.

'What the fuck have you done? They think we're a couple of poofs!'

While I was rolling around on the bed laughing, he begged me to go back and explain that I was joking because these weren't the most tolerant of people and he was still owed money.

Reluctantly I went back to the bar and explained to Ron that I was kidding but later on, after a counter meal, I couldn't resist trying to hold Bulldog's hand while we were playing pool.

The moral: Don't stand between a fatty and his Picnic bar.

8

Do you reckon we'll get our bond back?

In this day and age it's very common for kids to stay at home until they are well into their thirties. It's something I would never have contemplated; I couldn't wait to move out and have my own pad. But these days, when parents let you do it with anyone under their roof and have Pay TV in your room, and when mums cheerfully embrace hormone replacement therapy to help them ride out the complete mindfuck for everyone that is menopause—I say, good one.

My first share house was a converted office block in Queensberry Street, North Melbourne. I lived there first with my mate from uni, Hursto, and Killer, who at the time was going out with Hursto's sister. Killer got his nickname during a boozy night at the Corner Hotel in Richmond. While propping up the bar, which is one of Killer's many skills, a bloke walked past and accidentally knocked the pot out of his hand. Enraged, Killer went off at the bloke, demanding that he buy him a replacement drink. The shell-shocked bloke dutifully did and an embarrassed Killer accepted the beer, saying, 'I'm sorry mate, I've never done that before. I feel really bad.' (Killer was a notorious tight-arse, and when he bought his mid 1970s Fiat 124 in a private sale he made the guy throw in his pair of leather driving gloves—which didn't even fit—and then made him drive down to the servo and buy him a full tank of fuel.)

When we moved into the house, Hursto's base for his mattress couldn't fit up the stairs so we put it in the lounge room where it stayed for the eighteen months we lived in that house. Three years ago I made Hursto finally throw that bed out, and as we chucked it out onto the street for council clean-up we made up a little song, 'If only the mattress could talk'; Hursto, the 1990s and the ladies were a very good combination.

We had two spare rooms and couldn't find any friends who wanted to move in, so we decided to advertise. To say we were underwhelmed with responses would be an understatement. The first woman who came round sat down on the high-jump crash mat that doubled as a couch/spare bed for when our mate Bulldog came to stay and shocked the shit out of us by telling us straight out that she was a prostitute, and no, she didn't do freebies. Well, not only was she perhaps the world's ugliest hooker, she certainly wasn't the ideal housemate for a bunch of guys doing first year university. No tick for her.

Next up, we had a couple attracted to the idea of sharing the 60 bucks rent between them. I was late home from uni and missed the start of the interview. Breezing in with a fag in my mouth I caught the tale end of the conversation about a cat.

'I fucking hate cats. Hi, I'm Tim,' I said, quickly shaking their hands and throwing my pack of smokes to Hursto.

'Well, we have a cat, that's not going to be an issue is it?' the girl snapped at me.

'Not from my end,' I quickly backtracked.

For the next ten minutes this pretentious couple wanked on about their share-house philosophy. 'Look there's one thing we'd like to clear up,' tonked the bloke. 'We've lived in houses where someone has said, "Let's all go to Chasers," (which was a massive nightclub in South Yarra at the time) and we've felt the pressure to, like, go to Chasers, and if we, like, didn't go to Chasers, like, people would be upset. So we like to do our own thing and not feel pressure to go on household excursions.'

After they left opinion was unanimous, we all hated them—but they were a marginally better fit than the prostitute and we were desperate, so Killer got to call them and give them the good news. They were keen to move in straight away but we delayed them for four days so we could have our housewarming party without her cat shitting in the lounge room and ruining the vibe.

For the housewarming we managed to find an old water trough that we placed in the middle of the lounge room and filled with ice and beers. The lounge room had two double doors that led straight onto the street and predictably quite a few people were hanging around at the front. Things went a bit pear-shaped when a couple of skinheads walked inside and started helping themselves to beers. Being a bunch of tough guys we decided the safest thing was to lock the front doors to stop them from coming back. Kicking back with a can and feeling pretty proud of our skinhead repellent techniques, I was shocked to watch a cherry-red Doc Martin boot come flying through the window as the door was kicked in. Luckily for us, the skinhead hurt himself in the process and hobbled off with his mate, and the party could go on without any further issues.

When I got up the next day there was broken glass, empty cans and cigarette butts everywhere—the house was literally trashed. Bulldog, who had crashed on his high-jump mat, looked up from under the couple of pizza boxes he'd used as a makeshift blanket and groaned, 'I need some food!'

I completely agreed and we popped up the road to the bakery to get a pie each and a couple of sausage rolls. Sitting out the front of the house at 10am in the morning Bulldog gave me the 'fuck it, let's have a can' look, and we cracked one while we scoffed down the sausage rolls.

With the hair of the dog giving us a calming glow, I saw a Falcon station wagon coming down the road with a trailer holding a bed and some bits and pieces of furniture. Then it dawned on me, today was the day that the annoying couple was moving in. As they came closer to the front of the house, Bulldog and I watched them take one look at the smashed-in front doors, the empty cans and bottles strewn across the footpath, and the cat-hater and his shitbag mate necking a beer, and they obviously quickly decided that the house wasn't for them and just kept driving … We never heard from them again.

With the rent mounting up, a solution was desperately needed. Salvation came in the form of a chap we nicknamed Cool Hand Luke. Cool Hand had seen our ad on a notice board at Melbourne Uni and decided it was time to leave the suburban family home. He was quite a serious young chap, the president of the Dungeons and Dragons club and doing a triple degree in Drama, Literature and Being Boring.

We knew things were going to be interesting when his folks dropped him off with his stuff and he recreated his teenage boy's bedroom from home, complete with a single bed ensemble and a rather snazzy Star Wars doona. If the house was quite a shock to his dad, who helped him move everything in, it must have been worse for his mum. She refused to get out of the car or let his eight-year-old sister come inside to check out his new abode. It was probably a good thing because Hursto, who had just started playing late nights in a rock band with his brother, emerged from his slumber at 3pm and came downstairs to show Cool Hand's dad how to drink Patra orange juice straight from the bottle while sporting half a mongrel with nothing but a towel around his waist.

That night, I cooked roast lamb to welcome Cool Hand to our joint, and everything seemed to be going fine as we smashed the contents of a 4-litre cask of red wine. Then Killer decided he'd have a gnaw at the leftover leg of lamb. Not Hursto's or my bag but standard practice for Killer. What was truly weird, though, was that after he'd devoured it like a cocker spaniel with worms, Cool Hand picked it up and had a go too. Not only was he sharing juices with Killer but he also managed to get lamb fat all over the lenses of his glasses.

The next night Cool Hand had a late class at uni so he didn't join us for a parmigiana at the pub. When we got home we found him sitting in the lounge room wearing a black cape, reading a Kafka novel, smoking a Wee Willem cigar and drinking a glass of port. Hursto retired to his room, as he did most nights, to play guitar while Killer and I put the weirdness to the side to help ourselves to Cool Hand's port. He'd only intended having 'a nightcap' because he had an exam the next day, but within twenty minutes we had him playing a ridiculous drinking game we called Suicide.

It was very simple—you just dealt out a playing card to each person and whoever got the lowest-value card had to skol. Yes, it meant that someone had to skol every round, making things very dangerous. Things were pretty even for a little while until poor Cool Hand had a horror streak, which forced him to skol five glasses of port in a row. He was starting to look a bit wobbly so we called it quits on the game and Killer walked up the street with me because I needed a pack of fags. When we got back, Cool Hand was standing in the lounge room like Gandalf in *The Lord of the Rings* drinking straight from the bottle and reciting something that I'm sure he thought resembled poetry. We managed to get him into bed and put a bucket beside him in case he spewed and then retired to the living room to keep drinking. Five minutes later we heard voices in his room, so we walked in to make sure he was okay. He was lying in bed, talking on the phone: 'Mum, why don't you go fuck yourself,' he slurred. 'I don't care about my exams, they can go fuck themselves too!' I grabbed the phone and put the receiver to my ear and heard his dad on the other end of the line. In a panic I yelled down the line, 'It's okay, he's just tired, he's going to bed now, gotta go. Bye!' and hung up. With him snoring within minutes, Killer and I decided to call it a night too.

The next morning I got up with a massive headache and went downstairs to see how Cool Hand was doing. His bedroom door was wide open and when I looked inside all his stuff was gone. His dad must have come and grabbed him and taken him home where it was a bit safer. We never heard from him again.

(A few years later, Hursto, Killer and I were dragged along to see a piece of experimental theatre at Melbourne Uni that a friend was acting in. The performance piece, which thankfully I can remember little of, was performed in a very small room to an audience of barely ten people. The intimate nature of the performance space meant the actors were standing less than a metre in front of you. As they streamed onto the stage doing some bullshit post-modernist reinterpretation of *The Cherry Orchard*, we realised that the bloke in the tight lycra bodysuit in front of us was Cool Hand. For the next two hours I don't know who suffered more, us, having to sit though this excruciatingly painful rubbish, or Luke, having to do a monologue while making his hands stretch out like a tree directly in front of Killer, who was giggling like a school girl.)

So, once again in desperate need of a housemate, Killer interviewed and accepted a guy called Kyle without Hursto and I even meeting him. When he arrived all he had was a bag, a single mattress, and tennis racket re-stringer. There were no real clues why these made up his only possessions or why he didn't actually have a tennis racquet that could be restrung by his device. He quickly made himself at home and Blu-tacked his certificate of merit from the Westpac maths competition to the wall.

Kyle didn't come out of his room that night and Hursto was teaching himself to play 'Crosstown Traffic' by Jimmy Hendrix on his electric guitar, so Killer and I went up the pub and monstered a few beers. We bumped into some friends and invited them back to the house after closing and stayed up drinking until 3am.

The next morning Killer got up to go to uni and found 50 bucks and a note pinned to the kitchen door with a knife. It said, 'You guys are a bit too crazy for me. I'm out of here. Kyle.' This guy lasted ONE night, and of course we never saw him ever again.

In a stroke of good luck, Hursto and I bumped into an old mate Haymey, who we'd played football with at Swinburne Uni. He was a fantastic bloke who worked at Ansett in the city and had a permanent five o'clock shadow. Somehow we managed to talk him into moving in and suddenly we had another housemate who embraced minimalism when he moved in with a mattress, a footy, a suitcase and a stack of hard-core porno mags. I was impressed that he wore a suit to work and every morning he'd iron a shirt in his jocks with a fag in his mouth, and then off he'd go to work, always leaving the iron on. One day he left for work in a pair of jeans and a polo shirt and I asked him whether he had a casual dress day. It was only then that we found out he worked in the call centre and he could wear whatever he wanted, but that he chose to wear a suit so he could pretend he worked in finance to impress the ladies at the pub after work.

Our house, despite its derelict nature, quickly became a social hub. One night, Tong Po, an old mate from school, came round to hang out. He fancied himself as a bit of a guitarist so he went upstairs to show Hursto a few of his best licks. While he was decimating 'Money for Nothing' on Hursto's Fender Strat, Bulldog, Killer and I snuck out the front, jacked up his car and placed bricks under his axles on all four sides. We waited rather impatiently for him to finally leave, and then locked the front door and raced upstairs to watch the action unfold.

Tong Po jumped into his yellow Corolla, started the car, put it into gear, eased off the clutch, and put his foot on the accelerator, but of course the wheels just spun, inches off the ground. Not knowing what the hell was going on, he revved the car harder and harder, drawing the attention of half a dozen elderly Italian gents who were playing cards in the coffee shop/gambling den next door. They piled out to see what the commotion was about, and one of them tapped on Tong Po's window and pointed at the bricks. We, of course, were laughing so much we almost fell out the window, especially when he got out of the car and took four or five goes to kick it off the stack of bricks, told us to get fucked, and drove off.

Things got even more interesting around the place when I moved into the smaller spare room, enabling Greggles to move in too. Greggles was a mate of my older brother's who, although not qualified, worked with mentally ill people. He described his job by saying, 'Basically, I take people who aren't quite right ten-pin bowling, and I politely ask them to refrain from masturbating on the mini bus on the way there.' Greggles had a massive problem with the price of drinks at pubs, so when he went out he used to take an esky full of beer with him and hide it in the bushes. Every time he needed a beer he'd go outside and smuggle one in.

He also had a major crush on a young girl we knew, Chantelle, who seemed to have a crush on anyone but Greggles. He was desperate to engage with her on any level until things almost came to a scary end on the way home from a party. We were in the back of his enclosed ute when the car stalled in the middle of a major intersection. With cars screeching towards us from both sides we looked into the cabin through the back window to see that he was giving Chantelle her very first driving lesson. No L plates, no skills, and no idea. We were lucky not to be killed.

It was around this time that I entered Hursto, Killer and me in the battle of the bands at uni. It was a no-brainer really: the guys were great musicians and 'born to try', Delta style. There were only two issues: we probably needed someone else to join the band, and then I also had to break the news to my housemates that they were actually *in* a band and that we had two weeks until our first gig. After softening them up with a few pots of Carlton, they warmed to the idea and had enlisted our mate Carpsy to play guitar. Obviously, because I was to be the front man despite my limited ability, the boys weren't going to take it seriously, so Hursto, normally a guitarist, was to play the drums, and Killer, who was the resident Kenny G of the house, was to leave his saxophone safely in its case and pick up the bass.

There was excitement in the house as we battled not only to write four songs but to learn to play our new instruments. The lounge room became our rehearsal room and the band started to take shape. Killer and I started the ball rolling with a tune called 'I Drive a Holden (My One's a Brown One)', which had the haunting chorus:

In it you may not shit your Jockeys
My brown beast was driven by Brockie!
I drive a Holden (my one's a brown one).

Our punk DIY ethic was in full swing as I picked up the guitar and played my only two chords and penned the anti feral/hippy anthem 'Fuck Off Back to Byron Bay'. And because we were living slap bang in the middle of the grunge era, we added 'We're Not From Seattle But We Still Wear Flannel', a song which consisted of that lyric and very little else.

Because Hursto was probably embarrassed that someone might recognise him in the band, deflecting from his image as a serious musician, the call was made that we should don wigs, costumes and sunnies, so we became an Oz rock piss-take band. Wearing tight Faberge jeans, Bali singlets and Barnsie wigs we would take on the persona of a band that, despite being stuck in the late '70s and early '80s, believed it was the biggest thing in Australia. Carpsy, although he was the only one who was playing his natural instrument, was struggling the most with playing the songs. However, he coined the name and after two weeks of rehearsal Black Rose fronted up on a Wednesday night at LaTrobe University for our very first gig.

To say that we were nervous would be an understatement and, as we gathered backstage, it dawned on us quickly that we were probably way out of our league. Our fellow competitors were dismissive of our shit equipment. Particularly Hursto's children's drum kit, which only had a snare, a kick drum and high hat. As we changed into our costumes and stuffed socks down our pants to give us that essential rock star look, the other professional-looking bands could smell blood.

The first band took to the stage and played a tight set of well-crafted pop, and they had the audience stacked with mates, who cheered them on. Then it was our turn. As we wandered on to the stage, and they caught a glimpse of Carpsy with his guts hanging over the top of his acid-wash jeans, which were tucked into a silver pair of moon boots, the crowd started to chuckle, realising they were into a markedly different rock'n'roll experience. Channelling a mixture of Robert Plant, Daryl Braithwaite and Freddy Mercury on Ritalin, I launched into our first number, a ten-second punk rock version of the old TV commercial: 'Don't wait to be told, you need Palmolive Gold … thank you!'

The crowd laughed and then applauded. The next fifteen minutes was a blur as somehow we remembered the words and how the songs went. The audience lapped them up, particularly 'Fuck Off Back to Byron Bay!' and we walked off stage a BAND.

Then we did what was to become standard practice for this outfit: we retired to the beer garden to talk about how awesome we were and barely bothered to watch the other two acts that played after us.

Boozed up and feeling like Mötley Crüe, we went inside for the announcement of the winner of the heat, who would go into the final. Standing at the back of the room we were speechless when we won, on the night of our very first gig. The rock and roll dream had begun.

I'd love to say that the fairytale continued into the final, but we did come a credible second. This gave us a spot on the compilation CD that the student union was putting out, so we got to head into the studio and cut a couple of tracks.

When the CD came out, there was nothing more exciting than having our own music on a disc. Everyone was stoked until Killer looked at the liner notes and saw that they'd called him Ken 'Killer' Marsland rather than his real name Ben. It was a constant source of amusement for us because it shat him so much, and he actually accused me of giving them the wrong name on purpose. Despite us rejoicing in a stupid little ditty called 'His Name Is Benny But Now It's Kenny' whenever he walked in the door at our house, it wasn't the case.

What *is* true was that four years later, when I got a letter from the editor of the *Who's Who of Australian Rock* asking for details about the band for our inclusion in the next edition, I couldn't resist and gave him the following: Ken 'Killer' Marsland—Bass Guitar. And that is how he is listed to this day.

Our house wasn't exactly the Hilton, as you can imagine, and had a pretty crummy outside bathroom and toilet. The tiles had cracked on the floor and in one place the floor had rotted to create a hole the size of a soft drink

Dad's Suzuki, well before my brother Stephen drove it into the wall of the house. Note our dog Ted to the right. He had an aversion to mustard woollen jumpers and couldn't look at me.

In the 1970s Mum and Dad went a little too far with the 'Walton's craze' and made us all sleep in the same bed.

Mum and Dad in Fiji, 1981. Flowers as an accessory were big that year.

Campbell, me and Stephen, just a few years before we decided to try killing each other after school.

Dad's Holden Wagon. Seatbelts not needed.

Family holiday snap, Mildura, 1975. Dad, who took this photo, desperately wanted us to be the Partridge family.

Our family home, before the renovations and well before I almost burnt it down.

Things were tough for us as kids, we only had one basketball between us. Because Stephen was the oldest he got to wear it in all family photos. (This is the photo Mum had on her desk at her surgery.)

Exacta windcheaters must have been on sale somewhere.

Fishing with the Teacher, 1988. Time to break the news to the world, this photo is a fake. I wasn't raking in a fish at all.

Wearing a Jag shirt and ready to rumble. All haired up like Simon Le Bon; little did I realise that I would interview him one day.

Mix tape anyone? Myf Warhurst and I get ready to play some tunes at our Safari Suit party, 1993.

Rosso, Killer, Haymy, Hursto, Greggles. Also pictured are either a couple of gatecrashers or two members of Faith No More.

Killer, Rosso and our wallpaper made of tea towels.

Killer, Haymy, Hursto, Rosso, Greggles … same party.

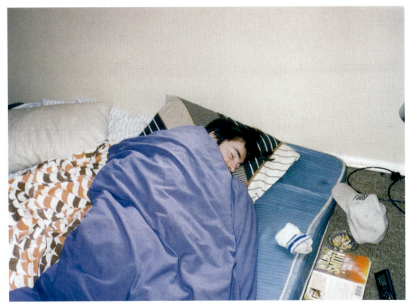

Haymy wasn't a big believer in sheets. He also loved smoking in bed and found eroticism in a place where few ever have, a Wilbur Smith novel.

Thumbs up for the newest member of the La Trobe Uni Alumni. Two universities, six years and 25K of HECS debt. One Arts degree, please.

Hursto, the ladies man of the
house . . . no, I can't see it in this
photo either.

Killer often dressed like a monk
to serve us drinks of an evening.

can where you could see straight through to the ground below. We asked the agents to get our landlord to fix it and they sent around a 'tradesman' who produced a large piece of 'waterproof' carpet that he used to cover the hole and tiles. Gee, didn't that make a difference!

One morning I got out of bed late and was surprised to hear Hursto in the shower. He was never out of bed before me but he was a bloke who loved a shower. He once said 'I'll have a quick shower!' and we timed him in there for thirty-five minutes. On another occasion, battling a killer hangover he took a plastic chair into the shower and sat in it snoozing for forty-five minutes.

After making myself a cup of tea, I heard the shower being turned off. I was still waiting for him to come in the back door when I heard a sound upstairs, and then Hursto himself came bounding down from his room in a pair of tracky pants.

'I thought you were in the shower?'

He just looked at me blankly.

'Well, if it wasn't you who the fuck was in the shower?'

I raced out the back door but the bathroom was empty, so I headed out through the gate that led into the back lane, and I saw an old dero scampering off, drying his hair with one of Killer's manky towels. The resourceful old crusty had snuck in and helped himself to our shower.

That winter we experienced a mouse plague of epic proportions. At one stage we were sure they were actually living in our fold-up couch. We would be sitting there covered in blankets and doonas (the house had no heating) and you could hear them squeaking underneath us.

I left a quarter of a hot chicken roll on a plate on the coffee table one night while I went up the street for ten minutes. When I came back it was completely gone, devoured by rodents (or maybe it was Killer?).

One impertinent little mousey walked across the top of the TV while we were watching *Fletch* on video. Instinctively, Hursto picked up the video cover and threw it straight at our unwanted visitor, hit it, and killed it on the spot.

We were pretty impressed.

We weren't exactly scared of getting delivery pizza and we used to stack the empty boxes in the kitchen— there would often be a pile of ten or so of them. It became apparent that this was a great food source for the mice and you'd often hear them rattling around eating the cheese and the oil-soaked cardboard.

I decided this was a perfect trap and I poured a whole box of rat poison into an empty box one night before we went to bed. The next day all of the green pellets were gone and we never saw a mouse again.

Everything went wrong with that house—locks broke, hot water systems packed it in, the roof leaked—and our landlord was never keen on fixing things.

Just off the lounge room, before you got to the kitchen, was a door that led to a cellar that continually filled up with rancid water when it rained. It had an automatic pump to remove the water, but it seldom worked and the stench of half a metre of water coming from under the house was too much to bear. But of course our landlord refused to fix it, so I'd often have to go down and wade through the muck to activate the pump by hand. The landlord, who we'd nicknamed Kinky for some stupid reason, was a lawyer and incredibly hard to argue with. He was intimidating when he came round and no matter how much we tried we could never convince him to fix anything.

Kinky also owned the office next door that one night suffered an electrical fault and caught on fire. Poor old Greggles woke to see flames licking the windows, got up in a panic, and woke Killer and me. We ran downstairs, quickly rang the fire brigade, and evacuated the house. It wasn't until the fireys arrived that we realised that Greggles had woken everyone but Hursto, who was still upstairs, oblivious to the sirens and the fire, getting his beauty sleep. I wanted one of the firemen to grab him and hoist him over his shoulder and carry him down in his Jocks, but there was little danger so Greggles ran upstairs and woke him up.

They put the fire out pretty quickly but because of its nature, a couple of firemen had to stay out the front and keep an eye on things for twenty-four hours, just in case it re-ignited. We didn't realise this until we got home that afternoon and saw them sitting there, bored out of their brains. Of course I told them they were more than welcome to sit in our lounge room, which opened directly onto the street, but unfortunately regulations wouldn't allow it. When we went out early that evening, I got an extension cord and moved the TV and video around and left our front door open so the fireys could sit on the pavement and watch it. We also set up the toasted sandwich maker and left some bread, ham, cheese and tomato so they could make themselves a snack.

When we got home after a fun night out, the lads were there, sitting on folding chairs, tucking into toasted sandwiches and having a right old time watching the *Godfather* on video.

The boys had used our house to run the hose through to access the back of the building next door, so after they'd manage to put out the flames, our house stank from the toxic fumes and everything had been affected by the smoke, particularly our clothes.

I rang the landlord at his office at 9am. Naturally, he was busy but his secretary suggested that we go and get our clothes washed at the laundromat and then they would reimburse us for the cost from their insurance. We washed our clothes but old Kinky the landlord never paid up.

When we moved on to another, better house around the corner, we piled up the stack of adult magazines that Haymey had kept under his mattress, put them in an envelope, addressed it to Kinky, and left a note with it saying, 'These are the magazines you and your wife left at our place. Cheers, Dave', knowing full well that his secretary would open it and there would be an uncomfortable moment for everyone. Hence our household's new motto: Revenge is a dish best served XXX.

Our new house was a palace compared to the old abode; it had a gas wall heater that we worshipped like a god.

After living for two years without any heating, we didn't leave our new house for weeks—it was pure luxury.

Although we were happy about our new pad, our arrival in the street was certainly an eye-opener for the neighbours. Greggles hadn't moved in with us—he'd bought an apartment of his own in Burnley—so our old mate Megsy had moved in, and then a little while later Bulldog joined us in the house too.

With five blokes and five assorted shitblock cars taking up extra car spaces in the street our neighbours on the left, who had a young family, weren't impressed from day one. The dad had a beard, drove an Audi, had an accent, and gave us death stares, so he was quickly nicknamed 'Scary German Guy'. We really got an idea of their lack of love for we boys when we were lugging band gear out of our house at the same time they were leaving theirs and we heard one of their small kids say, 'Look Mum, it's the drunkards!'

Unfortunately the young tyke was right. There was always music blaring from the house and people were constantly partying from 5am on a Saturday morning after we'd finished up at The Club. Hursto's band had a residency at this Collingwood institution and they started their set at two in the morning. Things got worse when the

Public Bar opened opposite the Vic Market; it was open until 7am. So everyone would leave The Club at 4.30, go to the Public Bar until 7, and then back to our place.

Black Rose did a residency at the Public Bar on Monday nights for the Fringe Festival and after the gig we'd take the cash, buy a few slabs at the pub, and invite everyone who'd been at the show to come back to our house for a party. We did this every Monday night for four weeks.

One of the Monday nights was particularly huge after a TV show called *The Times* came and did a story on the band. Hosted by journalist and author Paul Barry, the show was meant to be an alternative look at the news and aired late nights on Channel 7 for a short period of time. Having a TV crew film the gig was awesome and we thought this would kickstart the band to stardom. It wasn't until later that night, sharing a can with journalist/producer Mick Bunworth, that we learned the real reason they were doing the story on us. Mick admitted that he needed a Melbourne-based story so he could come down from Sydney to go to a mate's party—and it was a case of we would do. Mick came and saw Merrick and me when we did our first shows in Sydney and pulled Paul Barry along to the gig. A few years later Paul asked us to launch his bestselling book *Rich Kids*.

Obviously we had packed out the venue to look good for the cameras, so the party was heaving at our place after the gig. Our lounge room flooded with people dancing as Hursto and I played old disco records. If there was something to stand and dance on, then people were packed on it.

My girlfriend, who was notorious for going home early, kept ringing the house and crying, and ruined the party. It was impossible to work out what she was saying so I raced off to her house down the road to see what had turned her into a inconsolable mess. When she finally calmed down it became clear that she was saying, 'Rock Dog ate my corn!' I had left the best party we'd ever had because her housemates' dog had got into her vegetable garden and eaten her corn.

That wasn't the first warning sign that this one wasn't going to work out; she was also rather fond of weeing in the shower—when I was in there with her. Which one day found me saying, 'Can you hand me the Pert 2-in-1, please, and I see you've had a Berocca this morning.'

It wasn't just the noise that the neighbours objected to on these Monday nights. On the last one, our mate Juck had crashed out fully clothed on Bulldog's bed when the sun had finally come up. I thought it would be hilarious to use the smoke machine I'd hired for the gigs to smoke up Bulldog's room and wake Juck up. I set it up with the nozzle pointing through the slightly ajar door and took the remote control, which was attached to a 10-metre lead, up the hall with me. I lay on the couch and turned the machine on full, and it immediately started smoking up the room. Unfortunately someone had left the front door open and the old bloke next door thought the house was on fire. We had our second encounter with the North Melbourne fireys in just months when they stormed up the hallway to find Juck sound asleep despite the room being full of smoke, and then followed the cord of the still-bellowing smoke machine to discover me completely passed out with a stupid grin on my face and the control still in my hand, looking just like a petrified mummy. Well, so I'm told, because, like Juck, I slept through the entire visit. Thankfully they remembered us—and the toasted sangos— from the last fire and they saw the funny side.

As well as doing gigs in the inner city venues we started branching out to the country, picking up shows in Ballarat and Bendigo. These always paid well but the audiences could be very hit or miss. One Saturday night a venue could be packed with people who'd seen you before, but the next time, if there was a twenty-first somewhere or a big local footy game on, the crowd would be tiny.

Most times after a gig at the Bridge Mall Inn in Ballarat, we'd stay upstairs at the backpackers. Not that there were ever many backpackers there—it was more a place for recently divorced, angry dads and recently released jailbirds to kick back and explore their lack of options.

Once, after a rather kick-arse night on stage, I collected our money from the publican and asked about getting the keys for some rooms upstairs. Unfortunately, he explained, they'd had a lice plague and the whole of upstairs had been quarantined, so we'd need to find somewhere else to sleep. We had all been drinking and couldn't drive and there was no way we could afford a motel, so I enlisted the help of Deano, an old mate I'd done drama with at Uni, a talented musician, and a man about town. He told us he'd sort it and that everything was cool.

Relieved, we continued drinking, and when they finally kicked us out of the pub Deano took us to what we all presumed was his house, where we crashed on the lounge room floor, sharing a couple of blankets and a couple of cushions from the couch, with the heater going full bore to take the edge of the 4°C Ballarat night. Sometime in the morning we were woken with a jovial

'Who the fuck are you?' and it quickly dawned on us that we weren't at Deano's joint but in a house belonging to a complete stranger. As I tried to explain the situation to this poor bloke, who'd woken up to be confronted by six randoms sleeping in his lounge room, it seemed he only had a vague idea who Deano was. Deano, it seemed, was a friend of a friend who used to live in the house, and somehow he happened to know where the spare key was kept and let us in. Predictably most of us decided that we should leave as soon as possible. Not Carpsy though; he'd made himself very much at home and was enjoying a cup of tea with toast and marmalade, reading the paper while keeping half an eye on the unfolding drama.

That was pure Carpsy—a strange enigma of a bloke. A jazz musician with almost no knowledge of any form of contemporary music, he hardly knew what any of the lyrics of our songs were about (even though we were a comedy band that did funny songs), and despite being the one guy who was playing his primary instrument he was prone to being the sloppiest and most forgetful on stage. Despite that, this wonderful nerd, who wore old man caps and brown cardigans, who didn't have a TV and sat around at night reading the *Age* newspaper and listening to 3LO, was a dynamic performer. He'd take off his glasses, put on the tight jeans and Moon Boots, and bound on stage *sans* shirt to tear a room apart with his guitar heroics and presence. There was something strangely magical about being halfway through a joke on stage, only to hear everyone groaning and turn to see the sight of Carpsy happily squeezing pimples on his chest. For his first few years with the band Carpsy was still a virgin and he was often introduced as 'One of only two virgins in Australian rock'n'roll' (the other being Nathan Cavaleri, who at the time was a twelve-year-old guitar prodigy).

Obviously his virginity became a point of curiosity for the ladies, but Carpsy was a picky chap and was looking for Miss Right. He had a brief dip in standards during a two-night extravaganza we called 'Black Rose: The Miniseries' when a rather amorous and manky-looking forty-year-old woman decided to come on stage and dance dangerously close to him. The audience, inspired by yours truly, started chanting 'Pash for rock' and the demands of 300 people could not be ignored. Carpsy locked lips with this slightly insane woman and the crowd went wild. To paraphrase an old Rod Stewart song 'Some Guys Get All the Hep C'—thankfully he didn't.

Hursto was really starting to get the hang of the drums but was still prone to bouts of exhaustion. To combat this, he perfected the technique of vocal drumming whenever he was too tired to bash out a drum fill, he just sang it into the microphone like Michael Winslow, the sound-effect guy from *Police Academy*.

Jobs and university came off second-best in our house. Megsy, who was working as an accountant at the Water Board, took on the role of manager of Black Rose, and that public service fax machine and photocopier got a workout as he went into overdrive printing posters and fanzines and sending out press releases. We put ourselves into the Melbourne International Comedy Festival and decided it was time for a stunt for the media launch day. We hired a truck to drive down Swanston Street so we could play live on the back as we went along, just like AC/DC did in their 'Long Way to the Top' film clip. Unfortunately, Swanston Street is now closed to general traffic and only open to trams, cabs and commercial vehicles dropping off goods to the shops on the street. So, despite it being illegal, we gaffer-taped the PA and all the equipment down as well as we could with the help of our resident can-do man, PWS, and made our way down Melbourne's main thoroughfare with the volume on eleven. Within seconds people were racing out of shops and offices to see what the commotion was. They laughed, cheered and clapped as five ridiculously dressed young men played their hearts out. We drew level with trams, and passengers watched at eye level as Lordo, our dancing tambourine man, did the trick that never failed to get an amazing reaction. He stood on top of the cabin with his tambourine tied to his wrist with a piece of elastic. Then he threw the tambo 5 metres out in front of him until the elastic went taut and it came hurtling back. He caught it and the crowd went wild.

As we approached Melbourne Town Hall where the festival was being launched we had to drive past a police car. PWS stayed as calm as ever behind the wheel as we passed the boys in blue. But they smiled and clapped, which was a relief given we were flat broke after hiring the truck, and there was no way we could afford a fine.

As we got to the town hall, the TV news cameras and photographers all turned to us and we performed a whole song to the crowd that had gathered for the launch. Despite the great response from the media (we were on the news on all four stations that night), the organisers weren't very pleased; they'd organised a large group of traditional Japanese drummers (bizarrely doing a show at the festival) to play just as we arrived blasting out our wonky version of rock'n'roll. Whoops-a-daisy!

Inspired by the response, we reprised the performance for the Fringe Festival parade in Brunswick Street, where annually for the next four years we played for the 80,000 or so people who would gather along Fitzroy's main drag. It was always a buzz to see people hanging out of buildings singing along to our songs. Not that it was hard to be part of the parade: one year one of the most successful 'floats' was a bloke riding a bike with an empty Go Kat box taped to his head.

Cleanliness continued to be a problem in our house, and Killer's hygiene especially left a lot to be desired. One of his particular indiscretions involved a camping trip, an esky and some sausages. After taking a trip down the Great Ocean Road, he left the esky with the odd uncooked sausage or two in the hallway for a month. After constant berating, he relented and finally did something about it—putting the esky (still with the sausages in it) in his room by his desk, where it stayed for another year. Its existence became legendary, and friends often checked whether he'd moved it or not. It wasn't until someone decided enough was enough and opened the esky and plonked the year-old rancid sausages on his desk that he actually chucked them out.

More annoying was when he took my Breville health grill (a rather nifty electric barbecue) to a mate's house and brought it back filthy. After pestering him for weeks to clean it, I was alarmed to walk into our laundry to see old Killer scrubbing it with the dunny brush. In retrospect he can't really be blamed; we always assumed he had no idea what the dunny brush was because we were all damn well sure he'd never used it.

The peculiarities of the renovation to the old terrace house we lived in meant that the shower was situated off the kitchen and the door was right next to the fridge. This meant you had to walk through the kitchen/lounge room to use the shower. Bulldog famously opened the door into the shower only to find my girlfriend in there. He quickly closed the door as soon as he realised, but almost immediately opened it up again to take another peek.

Another time I was driving through the back streets of North Melbourne in my old Datsun 260C and as we drove past a girl walking along the side of the road Bulldog exclaimed in his typically laconic style, 'Look at the fat arse on that thing!' It wasn't until we got a bit closer that we both realised it was my girlfriend. He was mortified.

While we were all sitting around watching *Wheel of*

Fortune one night, Bulldog suddenly realised that Killer, who was walking past wearing a towel around his waist, had a striking resemblance to Ron Jeremy, a porn star nicknamed The Hedgehog for his rotund, hairy appearance. From then on, whenever Killer walked past us in a towel we would call him The Hedgehog—it drove him nuts. Megsy went as far as to find a photo of Jeremy, blow it up and make a poster with 'Killer is The Hedgehog' written on it. Then he stuck it on the back of the shower door just as Killer was about to go in. He wasn't suspicious when he didn't get the normal chorus of 'The Hedgehog' as he walked past us, but when he saw the poster he called us a bunch of cunts and ripped it off the door. We keeled over in hysterics.

In a stroke of genius Bulldog picked up the poster and taped it to the back of the hallway door, which led off the lounge room and was kept open most of the time. When Killer got out of the shower we stayed quiet until he got a few steps away from the hallway, then we all yelled out 'Hedgehog'. He promptly told us to 'Fuck off' and slammed the door behind him, revealing the poster—and we laughed even harder.

Amongst the visitors to the house over the years there was an assortment of young ladies, none more impressive than a woman who was starring in a major film at the time and who had taken a shine to Hursto when she went to see his band.

Word got round the house that this famous person had stayed over, and everyone was slightly jealous but also suitably impressed. Bulldog had taken it on himself to prepare an antipasto plate featuring some salami, Coon cheese and some stras (devon) just in case she got up and needed an exotic snack at 10am in the morning.

Needless to say, when she did get up and walked through the lounge room to see the four of us watching cartoons, the bong, and the amazing platter that Bulldog had whipped up, she quickly asked if we could call her a taxi. We all made pleasant small talk while she waited, and I naturally took the opportunity not only to play her a couple of songs from our EP but to give her a copy (it wasn't as if we were short of them; Megsy had 500 under his bed). When she left the whole house cheered and high-fived Hursto until we heard the doorbell ring. She'd left her jacket in his room and of course she'd heard us all cheering. She is now a Hollywood star.

When Bulldog reminded me of this story it seemed familiar, although in a completely different way, and someone pointed out that it was the storyline from *Notting*

Hill where the same thing happens when Julia Roberts goes to Hugh Grant's friends' place for dinner and she hears them cheer after she leaves.

The band was still mildly in demand and we agreed to play at our friend Myf's (Hursto's sister) twenty-first. It was a dress-up party, and we went and played as Kiss. We went to enormous efforts to look the best we could—we spray-painted girls' high-heeled boots to wear, and made a Kiss stencil so we could spray the back of our jackets and the kick drum. It was a fantastic night and despite murdering 'I Was Made for Loving You' and 'Rock and Roll All Nite' the band went down a treat. It was certainly a big nite for Killer, who was enticed back to a young lady's house in Preston. The magic ended in the morning when he realised he was 15 kilometres from home, his new friend didn't have a car nor did he have any money for a cab, and he was dressed as Gene Simmons.

At 10.30am, as we all sat around, seedily demolishing some Red Rooster, the call came: 'I'm in Preston. Can someone please come and pick me up?' There was a quick vote and the reaction was unanimous: 'Get the fucking tram, Killer!' So on he popped, eleven in the morning, hair tied in a bun, half his make-up still on, wearing a girl's pair of black tights and a black T-shirt with chains sewn on, wobbling down High Street cursing his housemates and debating with himself whether it was better to walk around without shoes or continue to wear a pair of spray-painted ladies boots two sizes too small for him.

The next time we played in Ballarat we didn't take any chances with accommodation and designated Megsy as the driver. After a so-so gig and half a dozen beers for the trip home, Killer noticed that, despite the road becoming more winding, Megsy's 1966 Valiant Safari wasn't slowing down and in fact was getting faster. Hursto and I were oblivious in the back until Killer decided to say something about it and Megsy suddenly confessed that the accelerator had been stuck for the last ten minutes and that no matter how hard he tried to brake, the car wouldn't slow down. This was a major problem because it looked like we were all going to die.

Killer watched carefully as Megsy put both feet on the brakes but we continued to speed above 110 kilometres an hour. Luckily, even though I'd been drinking I still had my wits about me and came up with a brilliant solution—all we needed to do was open the doors and jump out just before the car went over the cliff. My idea was sensibly pooh-poohed with a delicate, 'Shut the fuck up, Rosso!' and under Killer's instruction, with the motor continuing to wind up, Megsy dropped the car into neutral and then quickly turned the engine off, and thankfully, in time, we rolled to a stop.

Boys being boys, we gave the car a quick inspection and after a short test drive it seemed that the accelerator had fixed itself so we simply got back in the car and threw caution to the wind and drove home.

Not everybody hated us in the street. The old couple next door loved us because they were both deaf and couldn't hear a thing. She was lovely; she had a European accent and called us all 'darling', so we nicknamed her Zsa Zsa after Ms Gabor. One summer I noticed her husband wasn't around, and when I asked her where he was she told me he'd had a heart attack and was in hospital. A couple of days later I was sweating it out at the traffic lights in 42°C heat when I saw them walking across the road from the hospital. He'd just been discharged and these two old ducks, who must have been in their early eighties, had decided to walk the 5 kilometres home in the middle of the day in this oppressive heat. I swung round and told them to get in the car, and the old bloke (I'm at a loss to know why he didn't deserve a nickname), who wasn't looking too good, slid into the back seat. A few hours after I'd helped them inside, she knocked on the door and thrust a pile of gold coins into my hands. I tried valiantly to give them back to her but she wouldn't take them. Strangely enough it was some much-needed petrol money—as usual I was dead broke.

Most of the time in those houses we seemed to live in our own little universe, oblivious to the real world. After one particularly adventurous evening I found myself entertaining someone back at the house. At 8am in the morning and in desperate need of a prophylactic, I bolted out the front to retrieve one from the glove box of my car wearing nothing but a very skimpy '70s Playboy bathrobe that I'd found at an op shop. As I bent into the car I heard some voices, and when I looked round I realised that I'd inadvertently exposed myself to the woman two doors down who was taking her two kids to school. Whoops!

In a bizarre twist when everyone was finally moving out of that house, that woman went up to Megsy and told him that she'd been watching him for years, that she was extremely attracted to him and wanted to know whether he'd like to have a drink. Unfortunately he said no; I thought it would have been nice compensation for her walking right into a bird's eye view of my Jatz crackers.

9
Everybody should play in a rock band at least once

Nineteen ninety-five was an exciting time for rock, especially when it was your own band. We had just scored a four-week residency at Melbourne rock institution The Tote. This was a legendary venue: bands like Jet, You Am I and Spiderbait have graced its stage. Tragically, it recently closed down due to ridiculous licensing laws.

Like every struggling band, most of our following were our mates. Because we were pretty ordinary we had to keep coming up with inventive ways to make sure our 'fans' turned up every week.

For one of these gigs we came up with the brilliant idea of creating our own support band for an '80s-themed night. Not only would we branch out artistically but we'd also get to pocket the fifty bucks that the support band would get paid. As a result we formed Na Na We and billed them as 'Melbourne's premier Wa Wa Nee tribute band'. For those too young or lucky enough not to remember, Wa Wa Nee were a low-rent Australian version of Wham, with none of the hits and I presume none of the public toilet-based extra-curricular activities.

Despite our best intentions we never got around to actually learning any of Wa Wa Nee's songs. On gig day there was friction in the band when everyone refused to go along with my idea to just get up and 'make it up as we go along'.

Any of the unfortunate seventy-eight people who were in the crowd that night would have seen me and our manager Megsy (okay, he was our housemate who used the photocopier at work to print our posters) wearing bad mullet wigs and pastel-coloured girls' jackets prancing around stage miming to their one big song 'Stimulation'. So for fourteen excruciating minutes (yep, we played the extended 12-inch version) the crowd, too shell-shocked to boo, suffered through the one-and-only performance of the worst band to have ever played at The Tote. Yep, it's a big call, but I'm claiming it.

Years later we heard that the lead singer of Wa Wa Nee saw the gig advertised in the street press and snuck in the back to check out the show. Mortified, he later reported to his mates, 'It was terrible, just a couple of fuckwits dressed up like Jackie McDonald [from *Hey, hey it's Saturday*] miming to "Stimulation".' He was spot on.

STU

FF

Breaking up

If breaking up wasn't difficult, songs like 'Breaking Up is Hard to Do', 'You Don't Bring Me Flowers' and 'Who Let the Dog's Out' would never have been written. Much is made about the personal heartache involved when a loved one rips out your heart, puts it in the blender on full and then hits it with a Gray Nicolls cricket bat—but what advice is there for those who *want* to get out of a relationship? Those who dump are often saddled as the bad guy no matter which way it's handled. So I have collated a few handy tips to help you end a relationship by getting your lover to part ways with you first, meaning you remain the hero.

IKEA

Few healthy relationships can survive a trip to this home wrecker centre, let alone any that are a little shaky. Modern lovers aren't equipped to deal with paper tape measures, small grey lead pencils and objects with ridiculous Scandinavian names like Dugeverniushymen. If making decisions over which coloured furry bath mat to buy on a busy Saturday afternoon doesn't do the trick, cracking it and throwing a half-assembled coffee table against the wall will give them the impression that you're a deadset psychopath and send them packing.

Too much information

Ladies, if you really find yourself with a man you'd rather not be with, try this simple exercise. On a bright Saturday morning set an appointment in your Outlook and brightly declare, 'Oh my God, it's gangbang season!' When he timidly enquires what the *fuck* you are talking about simply reply, 'Every year when the sailors are in town I go down the docks and pick out ten of the best and have a great old time. This year you can watch, baby. Oh, what fun!'

Counselling

Nothing brings a rooted relationship to a head like a few sessions of overpriced counselling. Most people will go to relationship counselling to get their viewpoint validated by a third party. Unfortunately few counsellors will do this because fence sitting is the cornerstone of making you come back for weeks on end. You can get around this problem by getting a friend from work to pretend to be a counsellor. Then you just rock up to their house, they tell your partner that they are selfish and a destructive influence on you, and then prescribe a fishing/surfing/shopping trip for you and your friends, at the same time they gently suggest to your partner that they get their shit out of your house by the time you come back to avoid any more psychological scarring. To make it more realistic, the room should have a cat that stinks, a relaxation spa CD playing and a copy of the *Joy of Sex* lying artistically on the coffee table.

The way to a man's heart is through his stomach

So what are you waiting for ladies? Serve him up some dog shit on toast!

Set a cliché to ten

The reason they're a cliché is because they work. However they aren't quite enough to spell the death knell to most relationships. You have to soup them up to make them cut through these days:

It's not you, it's the internet

Create a Facebook page of you as a she-male called Cassandra, or leave your computer open on your blog entitled 'My life without a cock: A boy's struggle to live as a woman after surgery'. What was that? I think I can hear your boyfriend's car screeching out the driveway forever.

I just need a little bit of me time ... in jail

Pretend that you breached your parole by doing something nonsensical like attending A Day on the Green concert before you're forty, and that you're heading for the big house. Criminals might be sexy on the telly but not in real life.

I love you but I'm not in love with myself

Taking the concept of 'How can you love someone when you can't love yourself?' to an illogical next step, dazzle your partner with such assorted tales of self-loathing that they can't stomach your moaning any longer. To really push it over the edge, hold onto their leg while they are desperately trying to make it to the bathroom, and scream, 'Look at me! I'm horrid, even my toes are revolting. Somebody get me a saw, I want to chop them off!'

I just don't think I'm ready to not have a relationship when how can we be lovers if all we have never been is friends? I think I'm gay.

By the time they work out that this is rubbish they will dump you for being insane. Winner!

notrightinthehead.com

It might not have got Klinger out of the army in *MASH*, but pretending to be insane will get you back on the dating websites quicker than you can say, 'Can I have a glass of Tang with my Stillnox please?' When your lover comes home, surprise them by creating a shrine to the film *Fatal Attraction* in your study, with posters on the wall and the movie playing on loop on your computer. While wearing a home-made 'Glenn Close Rocks!' T-shirt, put a big pot of water on the stove and then innocently say, 'Honey, can you go and grab the next door neighbour's rabbit for me?' Mission accomplished.

The old disappearing act

If saying something like 'This weather is terrible for my herpes' to your prospective mother-in-law doesn't send your partner looking for a new apartment you may need to take some drastic action. This is what I call the old 'change your phone number, change the locks' trick, where basically you wake up one day and act as though they had never existed. Move all their stuff into storage and if you ever see them again simply look them in the eye and say, 'I'm sorry you must be mistaken. I've never met you before in my life!' If your friends play along with this too, not only will you be blissfully single again, but your ex will feel like they're living on *Shutter Island*.

1001 Musicians Who Should Die Before You (abridged version)

There is a myriad of compilation books out at the moment that list movies, places, books and albums that you should experience before you cark it. I know they look stylish on your coffee table and are fantastic conversation starters, but deep down they are designed to give you status anxiety, to make you feel like a tragic underachiever who really needs to get their skates on and do all these incredible things to impress a whole group of people that don't actually exist. I'm sorry if I've never seen *The Third Man*, read *Pride and Prejudice* or shat my daks in front of a sherpa in Nepal. I'm sure I'll survive. The thing is that nobody has actually done all these things, not even the people who wrote them. You might as well go out and buy a book called *1001 Reasons Why You're Not Very Cool and Haven't Made the Most of Your Life and Should be Embarrassed Because You Read the Da Vinci Code and Thoroughly Enjoyed It*. (And make sure you get the hardback version because it's more expensive.)

How can anyone expect to be able to afford to listen to 1001 albums? Even if you count illegal downloads and stealing some from friends, you are looking at least at $20,000 worth of music. Most people would prefer to buy themselves a Toyota Yaris and listen to the *Best of the Eagles* on repeat.

In an act of selfless revenge for the inferiority complexes these books give us, I present my own version: *1001 Musicians Who Deserve to Die Before You*.

Bono

Anyone who decides that he can solve world hunger by wearing a pair of girl's sunglasses and a flag made from a bed sheet is an A-grade wanker, no matter how talented. No world leader wants to meet you to talk politics; they just want their copy of *The Joshua Tree* signed for their stepkid.

Lil Wayne

My major problem with Lil Wayne is his name. The fantastic thing about being a rapper is that you can call yourself anything you like and people won't question it. Then you can change it again, just because you feel like it. So what's with that cat who changed his name from Dwayne—to Wayne. It's like saying I hate my name Craig so I'll call myself Craigo. And then when he does make the amazing switch, he adds Lil for credibility to be more like Li'l Kim. It must be incredibly hard to cap some homie in the ass if you've got a name that's straight out of *The Wonder Years*. Wayne is a shit enough name at the best of times but any gangster who has so many Waynes in his posse that he has to differentiate between Big Wayne and Little Wayne doesn't deserve a record deal.

Tracy Chapman

Tracy wrote a song about having a fast car called 'Fast Car'. The problem is that the song was a whiney soft ballad and she doesn't *sound* like she has a fast car, nor does she sound like she is the sort of revhead that's going to gun the bastard when push comes to shove. ZZ Top, *they* have fast cars, and they also know chicks with legs who know how to use them! Now *they* can be trusted with song titles; Tracy Chapman obviously cannot. She really should have called the song 'I Have a Licence'.

Chris Martin

I've interviewed this bloke a couple of times, and seen him live, and I'm pretty sure I own all Coldplay's albums, but none of my personal involvement in his career precludes him from being a nob. Perhaps it's his vegetarian diet, perhaps it's his unco dance moves, perhaps it's the fact that he can't watch *Fight Club* without imagining what his wife Gwyneth used to do with Brad Pitt, but there is something undeniably annoying about this man. As for him refusing to play the song *Green Eyes* because it's about an ex girlfriend—here's a newsflash for you, buddy, it's been a long time since anyone from The Kinks rooted Lola.

Black Eyed Peas

Since when has putting a metal colander on your head, wearing a pair of ski goggles and shoving half a roll of Alfoil up your jacksie made your music more futuristic?

George Michael

I say Bravo! to the man who made a million straight men dress like him in the late 1980s after the success of *Faith*.

Elton John

For years it was as plain as the stupid glasses on his face that Elton was as bald as a badger. Then a few years back he decided to try and fool at least a BILLION people by stapling what looks like an orange tea-cosy to his head. What was he thinking? Did he seriously believe if he wore hats and assorted fruit on his head for a few years that we'd forget he had a chrome dome?

Robbie Williams

Everybody loves Robbie; he's handsome, rich, funny and talented. Enough said.

Warwick Capper

Okay. Not strictly a musician but the one-time AFL full forward did release the woeful single 'I Only Take What's Mine' back in 1985. I always think of him in terms of that old Tom Hanks movie *Big*, where the ten-year-old kid wishes he was older and wakes up in the body of a man (Hanks). Only in Wazza's case, he's a labrador who's woken up in the body of a human.

Cliff Richard

When this lifelong bachelor falls off the twig don't be surprised if they find a Josef Fritzel-inspired rollerskating rink in a basement below his house, full of living dolls. If you'd never seen him before and he turned up with an acoustic guitar, you'd call the cops on the freak.

Susan Boyle

I don't think there's a person alive who wasn't moved by the footage of Susan Boyle singing on *The X Factor*. Her performance inspired a world that was feeling the pain of the global financial meltdown. It was a timely reminder of the power of humanity and proof that anything is possible. This, however, does not prohibit me from saying her new album is shit. I liked the old SuBo before she had the makeover and her bank balance exploded. Take me back to the time when she wore those dowdy old frocks, had those fuck-off eyebrows, and most probably, before waxing, she had a beaver the size of a toaster. The new Ms Boyle is plain annoying.

Lady Gaga

I interviewed Gaga once, and she was banging on about about how Kanye West was a mentor of hers and that he'd given her some 'awesome' advice which had helped her shape her career and make her the incredible artist that she is today. I immediately asked her exactly what Kanye had said to her, and she said that she couldn't possibly share that because it was private. She obviously has a weird take on privacy because she was wearing so little that I swear at one stage her vagina was trying to give me its autograph.

Sting

Sting has sold more albums as a solo artist than he did while fronting The Police. Sting released an album with the incredibly stupid title *Dream of the Blue Turtles*. Sting's gone bald and girls still think he's sexy. Sting's a proponent of tantric sex and can apparently have intercourse for seven weeks without stopping for food, water or an orgasm. I hate Sting.

Axel Rose

This snake-hipped rocker fooled us for years, hiding his red hair behind a bandana. If the world had truly known that he was a blood nut, I think we all would have agreed that he had an appetite for sunscreen rather than destruction. Welcome to SP50+ big guy.

Amy Winehouse

This skanky junkie is the first person to actually leave her body to science while still being alive. Research labs in the UK have spent hours trying to work out whether they are tattoos or scabs on her body.

Clarence Clemons

Just because he plays saxophone for the legendary Bruce Springsteen does that make him any different to Kenny G? The saxophone spread like legwarmers in the '80s, but thankfully organisations sprang up to fight the onslaught of this ghastly and horribly uncool instrument. Musicians like INXS's Kirk Pengilly spent thousands on expensive rehab programmes to wean themselves off their alto addiction. Please, Apple, create an application that allows me to remove Clarence's over-the-top sax solos from the Boss's classic *Born to Run* and I'll be a very happy man.

Bob Geldof

I saw earnest old Sir Bob on the telly the other day wanking on about being a pop star. Isn't it about time that someone reminded old Captain Hairy that his one hit song, 'I Don't Like Mondays' was released in 1980. Well done, you've also fed some kids in Africa, but for fuck's sake could you celebrate by having a shower please?

PART
4

10

What's an Arts degree got to do with it?

After three years living with the boys I started to worry about my degree. I'd been at uni for three years and I was barely halfway through a course most of my friends had already finished. I was having a great time but panic was starting to set in—I needed to knuckle down and do some work. I had spent the last year living in our second lounge room, which I'd converted into a bedroom with the nifty assistance of a wardrobe and a curtain. Whenever anyone came home they would basically walk though my room to get to the other living room, bathroom and kitchen and it wasn't exactly perfect for study. So I bit the bullet and moved into a house with Shosh and Jordo from uni, which was a much saner place to live.

I'd also got myself a six-cylinder mustard-coloured Ford Cortina for a thousand bucks. It was a three-speed manual and the fumes would come straight into the cabin and give me terrible headaches. At one stage, on most trips it would get stuck in first gear and I'd have to stop the car and crawl underneath and muck around with the gearbox until I clicked it out and I could start the car up again. After three months of doing this, and not having the money or the desire to fix it, I tried to sell the bomb in the *Trading Post*. Only one person was interested enough to come round and have a look at it and when he did I couldn't get the car started so he could take it for a spin. I think the words, 'Come on, you dog of a car!' were enough to put him off. It's entirely possible that car is still sitting in that street in Fairfield.

Study and I have never been great mates and to say that my efforts at tertiary education were mixed would be a gross understatement. My first attempt at a degree, a Bachelor of Business in marketing, had come to a grinding halt when the faculty decided that passing three out of ten subjects was not satisfactory and they threw me off campus. The Arts degree at La Trobe only went marginally better. I could never find it in me to attend classes or write essays: two of the cornerstones for successfully gaining a degree. The ridiculous thing was the extent I would go to to get extensions or be excluded from class.

One of my favourite tricks to gain more time to write an essay was rather elaborate. These were the days before email, so essays had to be physically handed in. I found out that they were happy if they were posted and I would take my cover letter into the Post Office, buy a pre-stamped envelope and then ask the person behind the counter to stamp my cover sheet so it would give the illusion that I'd posted it before the due date. I'd then write the essay at my own leisure, staple the cover sheet to it and then send it off. If I was ever asked where it was, I'd say I'd posted it and when the lecturer finally got it, the cover sheet was proof that it had been misplaced in the system.

Inspired by medical certificates I'd seen at Mum's surgery, I went to a dodgy printer in Preston and paid

150 bucks for a stack of fake ones. I'd made up the name of a doctor in Footscray—Dr Brian Theonopolous—and whenever I'd cut class and was facing failure I'd present one of these. They always worked. The only problem was that the accompanying anxiety that went with the fear of getting caught was so overpowering that I had to stop using them.

I was doing a double major in history, and theatre and drama, but it was the dramatic subjects that made up the bulk of my degree. I'd managed to stumble my way through Shakespeare in performance, naturalism and realism, women in theatre, Australian theatre and Japanese theatre.

In most cases there tended to be only one or two blokes in those classes and I almost got my head knocked off when doing a presentation on humour in the course on Australian plays. I'd used David Williamson's play *Don's Party* as an example. Set on the night of the 1969 Federal election it's an Australian classic, which Bruce Beresford had turned into a movie staring Graham Kennedy.

The fact that I'd admitted even liking a Williamson play was sacrilege to a few of those fringy arty types. However, things turned icy cold in the tutorial room when I used Cooley's greeting to Don of 'G'day, cunt features' as a most excellent example of a piece of quintessential Australian humour in theatre. Well, I might as well have hit Germaine Greer in the boobs with a tennis racquet because the Bundoora feminists went mad at me, accusing me of all sorts of crimes against women. There is no doubt there are moments of sexism reflected in the play but in this case I just found the Australian vernacular appealing amongst the sea of wanky prose that I'd encountered in the rest of this subject.

When one of the women in the tutorial asked whether anyone else thought the line was funny, I was thankful that the one other bloke in the class, Deano, put up his hand and said, 'Yes.' I'd just found myself a new mate.

Japanese theatre as a subject managed to find the perfect combination of boring and boring. Our teacher was an English bloke called Ian, who was a terrific guy, but his passion for masks and puppets had overtaken him. He was regarded as a world expert on Japanese Noh theatre and had written the definitive textbook on the subject, which had sold almost seventeen copies. Like most academics, he was taken aback by my sense of humour, particularly the day I bumped into him on a crowded bus on the way to uni and cheekily asked him whether he'd been done for DUI and lost his licence.

I really liked Ian but I just couldn't come at walking around the hall in bare feet, taking big, slow, elongated steps and repeating the line, 'I am Buddha, I am smiling'. Ian was big on warm-ups, which often meant a good half hour of stretching, vocal exercises or lying on the ground visualising that you were a seventeenth-century samurai—something I also called sleeping.

At one particular class Ian decided we'd dedicate the whole half hour of our warm-up to massage. This was a rather generous move on his part, I thought, as I was the only guy among a bunch of very pretty female drama students. It was going to be unreal. Even though I was excited by my potential pairing, I was momentarily distracted by a mate who was outside, wanting to bot a smoke. So I went out to give him one and decided to nail a quick one myself. When I returned, though, everyone had already paired up; without me in the room there had been an even number, so now I was partnerless. This was a disaster. But Ian quickly recognised my predicament and said, 'It's all right, Tim, you can partner me.' So for the next fifteen minutes under his instruction I massaged Ian's shoulders through his brown V-neck jumper, spending as much time as I could on the old Karate chop technique. Then we swapped and, despite his rather magic hands, nothing could fight the pain of seeing the girls' own magic hands all around me and knowing that I was missing out on the action. I can only think he was paying me back for that comment on the bus.

As the years rolled on and on at La Trobe, it wasn't just the band and my first attempts at stand-up that kept my focus from my studies; I was also enjoying doing student theatre that wasn't part of my course work. The student union had a bit of money to throw around for productions and I had a great time putting on comedy reviews and acting in the odd play.

Every year they would do a festival of one-act plays and ask students to submit pieces that they had written. If selected, a director would be found who would cast the play, and the production would then be overseen by a professional actor–director hired by the Union. I was as pleased as punch when they selected my evocatively titled masterpiece 'Who Left Their Cock Ring in the Shower?' a tale of the trials and tribulations of share house living. It was quite well received.

Another lot of plays we put on were chosen to be staged at La Mama theatre in Carlton. It was a fabulous little joint off Lygon Street and we felt so arty finishing up the show and then heading to Tiamo for a bowl of pasta and a carafe or two of red wine to discuss the night's performance. My then girlfriend directed the performance and had alienated us all by making us start the play in white lycra sacks that were already on stage when the audience came in. Hidden in one closest to the front row I couldn't help but have a chat through the cloth to Hursto and Bulldog when they came along. Of course this was scandalous behaviour on my part because I'd jeopardised the integrity of the piece and my girlfriend didn't talk to me for days. The only thing that broke the impasse was when I wrote off her Datsun 120Y on the way to the theatre one night. It's hard to keep up the silent treatment if you're cracking the shits about your boyfriend smashing your car.

In 1996 I was into what I was hoping would be my final year at uni. I was beginning to think that five years for a three-year degree was about right for me. Given that I'd blown another year at Swinburne, it was six years all up.

In the middle of the year I'd teamed up with Merrick, who I'd known from the stand-up circuit, and we'd produced a show called 'Pissheads from Outerspace' that had done very well and sold out its five-week run. I was working at the Student Union part-time doing publicity for a play, at the time, so of course I made sure I took the opportunity to use the facilities to publicise my own show.

Around this time Carpsy, our beloved guitarist, decided to move to Perth to give up the world of a rock god for the more fanciful life of a high school music teacher. There wasn't a dry eye in the house as everyone linked arms to sing a spirited cover version of 'That's What Friends Are For', and the crowd carried him off stage in tribute.

It was agreed that Carpsy was irreplaceable on guitar and so we never played regularly as a band again.

Towards the end of the year I started to panic about one particular subject—Australian History. In order to pass this unit, you only had to write three essays for the year. I'd written the first one but had missed the second one and it was time to do the third. I didn't know what to do; I couldn't do another year or half a year at university, I'd been there too long. If I failed this subject it meant dropping out, degreeless after six years. I was angry with myself for fucking up again. I decided the only thing I could do was go and see my lecturer. I explained my predicament, that this was the final subject that I needed to finish for my degree. My problem was that the second essay was months overdue and I pleaded with her to accept it. The only thing she said to me was, 'You can hand it in but I won't mark it'. This left me in a weird situation. What the hell did she mean? Was there any point writing both the essays if she wasn't going to mark the overdue one?

On the drive home I felt sick, I felt like a failure. By the time I got home I'd decided I'd write them anyway on the odd chance that a miracle might happen. I locked myself away for three days and wrote the two essays, making sure that at least the last one was in on time. I drove in and dropped them off in the essay box. My university work was over and now it was just a waiting game. The results were a month away but we were told that we could pick up our essays in a week's time. The drive out to get them was nerve racking. Did she take pity on me and decide to mark the essay? I raced up the hallway to the essay box and thumbed through the stack to find mine. I found the third one straightaway and she'd given it a C-. I continued searching for the other. When I found it my heart sank. As she'd promised, she hadn't marked it; it was there but not a thing had been written on it. Devastated, once again I headed home sick to the stomach. Writing those essays had been a complete waste of time.

Three weeks later I dragged myself to uni to check out the results because I wanted to know what I got for my two other subjects. The results were printed out and posted in the window of the admin building. I found my number and saw that I got a 68 and a 71 for my two drama subjects. Then I looked for my Australian history subject and saw my result—it was a 50. She had chosen not to mark it but she had passed me because I had bothered to hand my essay in. I was ecstatic; against all odds I had got my bloody degree.

Not that it has ever helped me get a job.

11
The dynamic duo

Of all the things Merrick Watts and I have shared over the years nothing has been more cherished by us than a small black bag full of wigs. Brilliantly known as 'the wig bag' it has been used in every live performance and TV show that we've ever done. In fact it was our mutual love of the comic use of wigs that drew us together in the first place.

On a rainy Melbourne Tuesday night sometime in 1994, I had a stand-up gig at the iconic Esplanade Hotel in St Kilda. Espy Comedy was held on Sunday afternoons and if you did well there you could progress to the more coveted Tuesday nights. Merrick and I happened to both be doing our first Tuesday night that evening.

I was a bit surprised when a big young bloke in a pair of flared cords and a Hawaiian shirt came up and introduced himself with one of the world's stupidest names, and then asked me how Black Rose was going. I hadn't met too many people I didn't know who'd seen my band, so that was a bit of a shock. He explained that he'd been at The Club in Collingwood when his brother Beech dragged him downstairs to check out this 'hilarious band that was wearing wigs'. He liked the show and had been a regular at our gigs ever since.

I was on before him, did okay, then I walked round to watch his set. He was brash and very funny and got quite a few big laughs. I thought he was hilarious. We hung out and had a few beers and I learnt for the first time that if you have a conversation with Mez, he does most of the talking. When the pub closed we went and got a souvlaki and exchanged numbers. I always enjoyed watching him do stand-up and when he took to the Punters Club outdoor stage during the Brunswick Street Festival in 1995, his set featured a routine about his rap mat, the piece of cardboard he took everywhere to breakdance on as a teenager. He was sensational. The hordes just stopped to listen to this twenty-two-year-old dressed like Rodney Dangerfield do his stuff.

Merrick and I used to catch up on Sunday arvos at the Espy and I got him to do some stand-up supporting the band on a couple of occasions, but it wasn't until 1996 that we decided to do a show together. Initially I'd envisioned a theatre-style show which we'd do from sleeping bags nailed to the wall. Thankfully, Merrick had no idea what the fuck I was on about and we decided on doing a stand-up show. I'd regularly drive to his house in Eltham after uni and he'd cook up a storm and we'd work on sketches and ideas. The more we threw ideas around the more we realised how similar our senses of humour were.

One of the things we did was write prank letters to celebrities and prominent people pretending to be small children or weirdo fans and asking them to write back to us. Who would have thought that if you wrote to Ronald Reagan as a child, calling him 'Ronald Raygun' and asking him what the TV show *Webster* was like, you'd get a reply?

We settled on the rather highbrow title of 'Pissheads from Outerspace' for our show and Beech, a graphic designer, knocked up a poster of us wearing bogan wigs with our heads speeding through space. I booked us in for five Wednesdays at the Rochester Castle Hotel in Fitzroy. The publican, Kenny, an ex-AFL umpire, was a true patron of the arts and gave us a $200 guarantee and then we took the four bucks off the door.

It was a fatal mistake to get Bulldog to do the door one night because he couldn't resist the temptation of putting all of our $2 coins straight in the pinball machine, which was located directly next to where he was sitting.

The show was a mixture of stand-up sketches and the prank letters, which we put on to transparencies and screened using an overhead projector so people could see them. These letters got a response like nothing else either of us had done before.

Obviously neither of us owned an overhead projector so I 'borrowed' one from La Trobe University and nicknamed him Fonzie … actually, I'm pretty sure we still have Fonzie.

We also started mucking around with shooting sketches on video. I had perfected editing—using pause, record and play—with a camera and a VCR. Spurred on by the success of our prank letters we thought we'd take it one step further and do something that we called 'Celebrity BBQ' where we'd find out where famous people lived and drop over unannounced with a packet of snags from Woolies and half a dozen beers. Merrick knew where John Farnham lived so we drove round to do a bit of a recky. The house was on a massive block and had a large brick fence and enormous metal gates. As we struggled to see up to the house, Merrick swore that he saw Whispering Jack and his flowing blonde locks getting out of a red Mercedes. Rather than front up straight away, Mez thought it would be best if we left a note in the letterbox, explaining that we were young comedians and that we were wondering if we could rock around for some snags and a few cold ones, leaving Mez's phone number. The next morning he got a phone call from a very irate woman, stating quite clearly that Farnsie didn't live there, had never lived there and we weren't welcome under any circumstances to 'rock up' with half a dozen cans of VB. It seems that it was the lady of the house rather than Farnsie we saw with the blonde locks getting out of the red Merc.

The show started gaining momentum and by the third week the venue was packed. Friends whose arms I used to twist to come to gigs were actually excited to turn up. Even better was that we were making a couple of hundred bucks each, which was incredible. After the show we'd head up to Brunswick Street, get a souvlaki and then head down to the Punters Club and have a few black and tans and talk about the show. It was such a rarity for us to have money in our pockets that we felt that we were really living it up.

By the end of the season there was a bit of a vibe out there.

Our next set of shows, 'The Imposters', at the Rochester Castle also did well and we set our sights on the 1997 Comedy Festival. The poster for our first show had read 'Merrick and Tim Ross'. Merrick was a single-name comedian like Jimeon but when people read the poster they thought we were brothers. So for the next show we changed it to 'Merrick and Rosso' which, of course, has stuck.

Despite the setback to our first attempt at 'Celebrity BBQ', we kept mucking around with the video camera. Given Mez's past as a breakdancer, we thought it would be fun to turn up at places and pretend to be from a fictional dance academy called Rap It Up Dance School. Dressed as if we'd just stepped out of *Breakdance Two: Electric Boogaloo*, with a dodgy letterhead in our hand and with a mate holding the camera, we lobbed up at Wesley College, one of Melbourne's most exclusive private schools. Somehow we managed to convince them we'd been booked for an appearance, so we set up the boom box and did a show for the kids in the quadrangle at lunchtime. Inspired by our success we went across the road to the Dance Centre at the Victorian College of the Arts, walked into a dance studio and again put on a performance for twenty-odd bemused students.

When we cut the film up and played it on the big screen to the audience at the Prince Patrick Hotel, the vision of one of the women from the VCA admin office walking up and saying, 'Excuse me, what exactly do you think you're doing here?' brought the house down.

Chris and John, the two Greek brothers who owned 'The Pat' were absolute classics. They lived above the pub and there was a rumour that, although they were both in their forties, they shared a bunk. It was probably true because their elderly parents lived up there too. The Pat was a wonderful venue for comedy and when it was full and going well there was no place on earth you'd rather be than on that funny little stage.

Chris and John's father, a tiny grey-haired bloke of eighty, used to come downstairs and make his way through the crowds to pour himself a pot of Carlton. After one of our shows John was having an argument out the front with a recently hired bouncer. Not liking the tone that his new boss was using, the bouncer pushed John in the chest. Suddenly, out of nowhere, the pensioner stepped into play. The old bloke decked the bouncer with one punch. Then he started yelling at him in Greek and kicking him with his Grosby slippers. He might have been eighty but it took both Merrick and me to drag him off the bouncer and inside.

Our Comedy Festival show sold out and got great reviews, and we'd got a good boost from an appearance on the 'Ladies Lounge Drive Show' on Triple J, hosted by Judith Lucy and Helen Razer. They'd loved our prank letters and had given us an open invitation to come on again when we next had a series of shows.

In July, when we returned to The Pat for a new season of 'The Merrick and Rosso 5000', another appearance on the Drive Show helped fill the venue to the brim and for the first time people were ripping our posters off the wall and asking us for autographs. When it happens for the first time, you really think someone is taking the piss.

During these shows we continued to muck around with prank calls. Initially I had a cardboard box filled with two sections of foam. We would take the telephone handset and line it up with a speaker and the microphone in the box and then tape it up. This primitive device took what we were saying from the desk and fed it through into the speaker in the box, which then 'talked' into the handset. When the person on the other end talked back, they were effectively talking into a microphone going through the PA. Surprisingly it worked well. For one of the shows we decided to put an ad in the paper for a room for rent in a share house. To make sure we got loads of responses our ad read like this:

> Room for rent in Richmond house. Ensuite
> bathroom, off-street parking, pool, tennis court,
> sauna. $50 a week. Call——after 9 on Wednesday
> night.

Well, the phone rang off the hook with people wanting to move in and we put them through a ridiculous screening process. 'Do you like Weetbix?' 'You do? Sorry we're looking for someone who hates Weetbix. Sorry, goodbye.' After letting a guy go because he couldn't play the French horn, he rang back so angry that we had to tell him it was a joke and that he was part of the show. We offered to shout him a beer if he came down right now and just before the show finished he blustered through the front doors to a thunderous round of applause.

Later on, James, the sound guy at The Pat, made us a rather nifty device from a hands-free unit which enabled us to do prank calls from a mobile through any PA as long as there was mobile phone service. It came in very handy.

We were still having great fun shooting hidden camera stuff. I'd noticed there was going to be a shopping centre appearance by the cast of *Neighbours* so we decided to dress up as rather special fans complete with our own homemade 'I Love Helen Daniels T-shirts' and made our way up the front of the stage and screamed the most bizarre things we could think of as we stood among a sea of screaming twelve-year-olds. It's amazing how, if you are wearing a beanie and have your tracksuit pants pulled up to your tits and if you ask them for long enough, it seems you really *can* make a soap star bark like Bouncer into a microphone.

I think we were enjoying this a little too much.

A video where we dressed up as bogans and visited the newly opened Crown Casino was very popular at the live show, and Sharon Scrase, a producer at Steve Vizard's production company asked us for a copy. Not having the facilities to dub one we drove down to their offices in Port Melbourne and she did it there.

Everyone at the production company liked it and they asked us to do small series of ten similar videos for the Comedy Channel at Foxtel. This was a great opportunity. An episode where we dressed in green 1970s deb ball suits and gave Nicole Kidman a copy of *BMX Bandits* to sign at the Australian Film Institute awards gained us a little bit of media attention. In that particular episode a young—and much thinner Matt Preston—stopped to talk to us on the red carpet because we were all wearing white dress shoes.

Another in which we went to the Botanical Gardens in overalls, hard hats and carrying chainsaws and asked people to move from beneath 100-year-old trees because we were about to cut them down because 'they'd been dropping too much shit' and 'were causing too much shade' became a favourite when we played it at live shows.

We were pretty excited about working for Vizard, even more so when were invited to the Artist Services Christmas party at his house. When we arrived they had shots of tequila and that gave us a good taste of what was too come. Being struggling comedians, free booze was a big thing and we certainly made the most of it. It was wall-to-wall celebrities like Eddie McGuire, Sigrid

Thornton and Deborah Lee Furness. After an hour of solid drinking I was ready to say 'Hi' to a few of them. Aussie actor Steve Bisley was the first on my radar. I'd bumped into him at a King Street nightclub when I was eighteen and, being a cocky young chap with a few drinks under my belt, I told him to remember my face because one day we'd meet again when I was famous. I thought this was the perfect time to remind him of this story because I had a five-minute TV show on Foxtel and I was killing it! He, of course, thought very little of my extremely shit story and walked off. I thought that he hadn't understood it properly so I went after him to tell him again and again. After that I made my way inside to say 'G'day' to Vizard and let him know that I thought he was a legend. I told him that he was like Graham Kennedy to me and then I patted him on the arse—as Merrick so eloquently puts it—'like he'd just kicked a goal for Collingwood!' Steve wasn't impressed. I was just about to retell my story to Bisley again when I spotted Sigrid Thornton. On the words, 'Let's go talk to Sigi', Mez decided it was time that I went home.

The next day I woke up with the biggest case of booze anxiety known to man. I picked up the phone and rang Mez.

'Tell me honestly—do we still have a career?'

'I don't know.'

It was a nervous wait over the weekend to see whether there was any fallout and then on Monday morning we got the news. Thankfully, after I'd left, a very well-known male actor had spewed in Steve's lounge room all over the brand-new rug and lounge. He had taken the heat off me. I was fine.

We really enjoyed doing the little show *Planet Merrick and Rosso* for Artists Services and they were impressed that we were always down at the edit suite getting involved in the way the show was cut. As much as I'd like to say that we were that conscientious, Jason the editor was all over the job and needed little guidance; we just went down because they bought us chicken schnitzel sandwiches.

Our next adventure was a three-week season at the Harold Park Hotel in Glebe. This was our first interstate jaunt and from the outset I loved being in Sydney. It was September, the weather was fantastic and the girls were so pretty I found its sexiness intoxicating.

We elected to take a larger fee and stay upstairs at the pub. There were some interesting characters living upstairs and we'll always be eternally grateful to them for the extremely ferocious strain of tinea that we both contracted in the shared bathroom.

After our first night we hit the schooners hard and were in pretty bad shape the next day when we were to head into Triple J for another spot on the Ladies Lounge. At one stage Mez had to lie down in the gutter on his way back from getting some breakfast on Glebe Point Road.

Around about 2pm I finally stopped being sick and we got a cab into Harris Street for our interview. Despite the state of our health, we were in surprisingly fine form and got some great jokes away. That show was Judith Lucy's last; Helen Razer was going to continue on alone. As soon as we got off air, management asked us to do a regular weekly spot with Helen. This was an incredibly important break for us.

It certainly helped with our Sydney season; so did an article in the Metro lift-out of the Friday *Sydney Morning Herald*. They published a prank letter that we'd written to John Howard as if from a small kid. In it I asked him if he knew the Rank Donkey Dance, there being no such thing of course. The Prime Minister had replied and rightfully admitted that he didn't know the dance.

I took the opportunity to ring talkback station 2UE and found myself on air with Ray Hadley, who was filling in for John Laws. I complained loudly about how offensive I found the letter in the paper, Ray not only read out the letter and the response in its entirety but he gave out the tour dates as well.

The call ended with, 'You know what this is, Ray? It's a waste of taxpayers' money!'

'I agree,' he replied.

Merrick recorded the whole call on a tape deck in the public bar of the pub and we couldn't wait to take it in and play it on the radio. Triple J had opened up the country for us and we spent the next year touring our new show 'Mardi Grouse' everywhere.

Two mates telling jokes on stage—they were great times.

MORE STUFF

→

STU

FF

Kids

It seems to me that people today are far more judgemental about parenting than ever before. Judgements are made on what people feed their kids, how often they do or don't go to childcare, how often they're read to, when they start swimming lessons ... and the list goes on. Now don't get me wrong: I once came close to calling DOCs when a relative brought their kid to a family barbecue in a pair of orange Crocs (those things are the work of Satan), but isn't it time everybody lightened up?

If you go to a kid's party these days the kids aren't allowed sugar. Nothing more annoying than turning up to a friend's kid's birthday party with a massive hangover, ready to murder a glass or two of lime cordial, only to be presented with a glass of water and a carrot stick. Isn't the joy of a birthday party about dropping your kid off for a few hours, letting them OD on sugar,

then picking them up when they're thoroughly
exhausted from decimating a row of agapanthus
with a broom handle?

When I was a kid the only time I can remember
the oldies laying judgement was expressing some
mild disapproval when I had dinner at a friend's
place and they served up Deb instant mashed potato
instead of the real thing. I think Mum might have
questioned why you needed to use dehydrated potato
flakes in a packet when it only takes a couple of
minutes to peel a few taties. The irony is that
no-one even blinked an eyelid when my mate's Dad
had dropped me off in his V8 Ford Cobra Coupe
with a can of Fosters wedged between his thighs.

In these times when old jokes like 'I love kids
but I could only eat a couple of them' could see
you arrested for being a paedophile, I'd like to
share a couple of children's stories that I wrote
for a close friend's kids. Sure, I would have
loved a separate publishing deal for my kids'
books, but I think I've been lucky enough to get
one deal away, so I'm making the most of it.

Uncle Timmy and his magical bottom

It was a cold winter's Saturday afternoon and
Uncle Timmy and Daddy had been at the club for
a few hours catching up on some very important
stuff. When they came home they were smiling and
in a funny mood. They both smelt of garlic because

they'd had a kebab on the way. While Mummy went for a drive to calm down, Uncle Timmy and Daddy sat on the couch while we played with our dolls. We had all of them lined up but I couldn't find my favourite, Sarah, anywhere. Suddenly I realised that I'd left her on the couch and Uncle Timmy was sitting on her!

'Uncle Timmy, you're sitting on Sarah. Get off her quickly,' I said.

'Who's Sarah?' he asked.

'She's my favourite doll, who has realistic hair that can be blow dried just like real Hollywood celebrities!'

'Wow, I think I've found her!' he said, but just as he adjusted himself to grab Sarah he let rip a big fart!

We all laughed because it was always funny when Uncle Timmy 'dropped his guts', as he put it. But while we all giggled we heard a little sound.

'Help me!'

What was that? Where was it coming from?

'Help me!'

There it was again. We all stopped and looked around.

'Please get off me, you're hurting me!' came the little voice again—and it was coming from the couch. I looked down and the little voice was coming from under Uncle Timmy. I pushed him out of the way; I couldn't believe it, there was my Sarah, looking up at me smiling!

'Sarah! Are you okay?' I asked. 'Uncle Timmy didn't hurt you, did he?'

'No,' she said, rearranging her supertight disco jeans. 'I'm fine. It's just so nice to be alive!'

Daddy and Uncle Timmy were in shock; they couldn't believe my doll had come to life!

'Crikey, little lady,' Uncle Timmy said as he bent over to take a closer look at Sarah. 'You *are* alive! How did that happen?' And as he said that, his bottom let out another blast.

'Pwoah, Uncle Timmy!' we all yelled, and then we heard another little voice coming out from behind him,

'Excuse me, do you have any honey? I'm starving!' Now Keithy, my big brown teddy bear, was talking too!

'How did this happen?' I asked again, as Teddy started walking towards the kitchen looking for a snack.

'It's Uncle Timmy,' said Sarah. 'His fluffs have magically brought us to life!'

'Must have been the chilli sauce on that kebab!' said Daddy.

Uncle Timmy was looking puzzled; I don't think he could believe that his stinky pop pops could have done it.

'I'm not sure about this. I think we need to put it to the test,' he said. 'Hand me that pony!'

Mum had a Kingswood

I handed Uncle Timmy Jezebel, my favourite pony; she has such a pretty mane. As soon as he had it in his hands, he put it on the chair, perched his bottom over her, and screwed up his face, desperately trying to back one out!

'You be careful,' said Daddy. 'We don't want any accidents!'

'There won't be any accidents. I'm a professional!' was Uncle Timmy's reply as he promptly fluffed on demand—and lo, and behold! Jezebel the pony started cantering around the chair Mum bought from IKEA.

'Oh Uncle Timmy, your bottom is really magical! What else can you bring to life?' I screamed with joy.

'Gee. I don't know ... let's try that car?'

And so it began. Uncle Timmy fluffed on all our toys and they all came to life. Sarah talked to me about having plastic arms; Teddy ate the honey straight from the jar; and Jezebel ate some grass from Daddy's special tin which made her very sleepy.

We had so much fun; we didn't even mind that the house was really stinky with the smell of Uncle Timmy's cheek flappers. But after 15 minutes something strange happened: one by one the toys stopped moving, they were no longer magically alive.

'What's happening, Sarah? What's happening to you?'

Little Sarah, her arms stiffening in front of her, looked up at me, 'It's the fluffs. When your Uncle Timmy's fluffs stop smelling we go back to being normal toys.'

'But what can we do? I want you all to stay alive ... well, maybe not Jezebel, she's gone insane!' I cried.

'Feed Uncle Timmy beans!' she weakly sighed as she turned back to her original state.

'Quick! To the kitchen! We need to feed him beans, beans always make you launch the best undie-rippers!' yelled Daddy, as he raced to the kitchen.

Then we heard the front door open and Mummy came storming down the hallway.

'What are you up to now?' She said, glaring at Dad and Uncle Timmy!

'Mummy, Uncle Timmy's bottom has magical powers. He did a pop off on my toys and they came to life, but they only stay alive while his fluffs are stinky, so we're making some beans to make him fluff again!'

'Oh what rubbish! I'm not having you doing that to her toys! It's unhygienic! It's time for your bath—and its time for Uncle Timmy to go home!'

'But Mummy, Sarah hasn't finished telling me what it's like to be made in China or what it's like to have feet that are designed only for wearing high heels.'

'That's enough, young lady. The games are over. Uncle Timmy is a drunk, your Father is easily led, and I've got my period, so it's off to bed with you before I really lose it!'

I hadn't seen Mummy that angry since Daddy went to the Gold Coast for a night with Uncle Timmy and came back four days later. I didn't want to upset her any more, so I grabbed Sarah and went to my room. I sat in bed looking at Sarah, wishing that she could talk to me again.

There were voices in the hallway, and then Daddy and Uncle Timmy came into my room.

'Uncle Timmy wants to say goodbye,' said Daddy.

'I've got a present for you,' said Uncle Timmy. And he presented me with an empty Vegemite jar.

'What is it?'

'I managed to crank out a few beauties and I popped 'em in a jar for you, sweetie! Whenever you want to talk to your dolls, just lift the lid, let 'em have a whiff, and they'll come alive for you.'

'Oh, Uncle Timmy, I don't care that Mummy thinks you're a pathetic drunk with self-esteem issues and a gambling addiction—I think you're the best uncle in the whole wide world!'

I was so tired as I put the jar on my bedside table, but I was also really excited that when I woke in the morning I could bring my toys back to life once again.

Almost Twilight

I like the idea of having balance in this book, something for all ages, so here I present something aimed specifically at the teenage reader. From what I can tell most teen fiction is written by Volvo-driving mums who eavesdrop on their teenage children's conversations and then as soon as the kids are at school crack a bottle of sauv blanc and hit the keys.

Well, if you can't beat them join them, I say. It's white wine time.

Katie took a glance at her Motorola Razr phone—still no messages! Brian had promised that he'd let her know as soon as he'd finished footy training. Most of the girls at school thought Katie was a moll for thinking about going 'all the way' with Brian but she was sure that she loved him, and after going out with him for three days it was definitely time.

Mum had a Kingswood

She had only been at Fresh Suburb High for half a term but on the whole she had settled in pretty well. It had been tough leaving Queensland with her mum, but after her dad had gone to jail for murdering her principal it was for the best. She tried to block out that day when her dad had strangled Mrs Kennedy with a GHD because she wouldn't let Katie take a day off school to go to Brisbane for the science fiction and fantasy expo, even though Katie would have had the chance to get an autograph from a few of the lesser known stars of the *Twilight* movie.

A few sessions of therapy with the school counsellor and the excitement of having a hot new boyfriend had awesomely kept her mind off the thought of her dad being raped in the big house.

Suddenly her phone beeped, it was a text. She opened it.

'u r a slt lol!'

Ha ha! It was from her best friend Candice; she was such a hoot. She couldn't believe she'd found a BFF like her in such a short time. They had so much in common: they both loved playing 'Dance, Dance, Dance Nation' at Timezone, watching *Glee* and they also used the same Libra product, so they were practically sisters.

'where u?' She replied on SMS.

And within seconds came her reply.

'riding Justin beiber he feels gr8! lol.'

Katie laughed and she wished it was true. Candice and the teen heartthrob would certainly make a cool couple. Suddenly she got sad again. That darkness came over her and once again she fought back the tears: 'What happens if I don't get a job on *Home and Away* when I finish school?" She pushed back such horrible thoughts; she could always audition for *Neighbours* couldn't she?

Feeling much better, Katie went to the pantry, got herself a muesli bar and then went to the bathroom to apply a little bit more Clearasil to the large pimple on her chin.

'Trust me to get a massive zit on the day Brian is coming round with a franger and we're going to do it.'

Suddenly as she looked at herself she saw herself back in Queensland a few years ago. She was sitting in her bedroom playing with her My Little Ponies while Dad was watching the Broncos on the TV and Mum was locked in her bedroom with a bottle of Bundy.

They were happy times, but now she has grown up and she no longer has My Little Ponies, but she does have a boyfriend who wears baggy Quicksilver jeans, rides a skateboard, and knows all the lyrics to Guy Sebastian's new album. He was positively dreamy.

She wondered whether she should tell her mum about Brian. She pretty much told her mum about everything! She looked at the book on the kitchen bench. It was a present for their next-door neighbour Hassan. She looked at the title *Are you there Allah, it's me Abdul!* It looked like a stupid book but it was nice of her mum to get him a present for his sixteenth birthday.

Next year was her sixteenth birthday and she was hoping to have the biggest party, or maybe she'd just do something intimate with Brian like go out for tea at the local café where she'd have fettuccine and an orange Bacardi breezer and Brian would have lasagne and a Pure Blonde. That would be the best birthday ever.

She wondered if Pop would send her a card from the Philippines. She hoped that she could go and visit him as soon as she finished school; she'd love to see the bar he owned in Manila. Maybe if she kept up her dance lessons, she could dance with the other girls there. It would be just like that movie *Fame* but instead of a performance high school in New York, she'd be dancing on tables in South-East Asia.

Still no text from Brian! Her mind raced again, what if he was secretly gay? Bradley in Year 11 was openly gay; they'd done the rock eisteddfod about it with him in the lead. There had been a massive argument about what song to do. Mr Begg the drama teacher wanted to stage the number 'I Want to Break Free' by Queen but the students wanted 'Rock with Me' by Justin Timberlake.

They'd compromised and done a mash-up of the two songs. They symbolised Bradley's struggle with his sexuality by having a tug of war between Paris Hilton and George Michael with Bradley torn in the middle. Most of the parents thought it was shit.

No, Brian couldn't be gay—he'd almost done it with Sarah but apparently she was frigid and she'd changed her mind. She was such a stuck-up bitch, just because her mum had made a fortune with Nutrimetics didn't give her the right to be so cruel to people. She hated Sarah almost as much as she hated her Nan for denying Pop his natural urges and making him leave them all.

Suddenly there was a knock on the front door. She ran and opened it and there was Brian, smiling and looking so gorgeous in his Tupac singlet, cut-off denim shorts, Nike high tops and *Deal or No Deal* trucker Cap.

'Hi Brian, you look so cute. What took you so long?' asked Sally as she leaned forward to kiss him.

Brian pulled away.

'What's wrong, Brian?'

'I have something to tell you, Katie', said Brian as he looked her straight in the eye.

'Oh no, it's not my pimple is it? You don't want to do it because of my pimple?'

'Oh, don't be silly!' he reassured her.

'I know! You googled Canesten after you found that tube in my room. It's my mum's, I swear.'

Mum had a Kingswood

Brian grabbed her hand. 'Katie, it's not that. The other day my friend Trevor took me to the Hillsong Church and I've discovered Jesus and as much as I love you I know it's against God's will for us to do it even though I've got a franger in my wallet.'

Katie started to cry. 'I'm so relieved! I thought you might be a poof who only likes bum sex, but now I know you have a friend in Jesus, I think I'd like to be his friend, too.'

Brian took her hand again. 'That's easy—he's ready to be everyone's friend. Let's go make out on your couch and rub against each other until it's so uncomfortable that I have to leave.'

'I couldn't think of anything I'd rather do, Brian.'

The end.

PART

5

12
ABC isn't always as easy as 123

I can honestly say that the two years I worked full-time at Triple J were the most fulfilling of my professional life so far. This strange little cousin to the more sensible radio stations within the Australian Broadcasting Corporation is certainly an enigma. With a signal that can be heard pretty much everywhere across the nation, the youth network with its focus on independent, interesting, alternative and local music sets itself apart from every other radio station in the country.

Sandwiched on level 6 of the ABC offices in Ultimo in Sydney, the Triple J offices and studios have always felt a bit like wonderland to me. With gig posters, gold records and boxes of audio tapes clinging to the walls and blocking the hallways, it's a music lover's dream. When I think of the music library with every album you ever wanted to own in it, I wish the technology had been available for me to sit with my laptop and burn away while I was working there. In the simplest terms Triple J's charter is to play great music (especially from Australia) and to create great content ... hell, who wouldn't want to be part of that?

The ABC is, of course, part of the public service and with the Js you get an even weirder sub branch that made for a very relaxed workplace. Nothing sums up the spirit of the place more than the day when everyone left the office and walked up Harris Street to the George Street Cinemas to attend a media screening of the second Austin Powers movie. I'm talking everyone—senior managers, the lot. We put the answering machine on, left Francis Leach doing the Morning Show from the Melbourne studios and the whole office emptied. This wasn't part of any thought-out team bonding exercise; it was just how the station rolled. It was a good movie, everyone wanted to see it, so we did.

People always seemed to be ducking out to the pub only to come back and have a little nap in the beanbag that most of the time was positioned in our studio and they'd be asleep while we were on air.

The J Van, the station Tarago, was a free-for-all. If you wanted to go home at lunchtime, move house at the weekend, or pick up some mates from the airport, the keys weren't far away. One weekend a couple of announcers borrowed it to drive to a dance party in Melbourne. Only later did they realise they had both bullshitted each other about having a driver's licence.

Some of the long-term employees had some pretty major perks sorted. One in particular had dreamt up her own industrial award and would take a rostered day off on the first Tuesday of the month. She had been doing this for ten years before someone realised that she'd conjured the whole thing up.

Around the time of the Big Day Out, the ARIA awards or Mardi Gras, working hours became super-flexible and staff would often be missing for days, but despite the good times people worked as hard as they played—if not harder—and made programs on the smell of an oily rag.

Once a week we'd have a music meeting where Arnold Frollows, the music programmer, would play any new music that had come in and we'd decide whether it would get on air or not. Arnold, who once worked in A&R for Virgin records in the UK, famously knocked back signing Dire Straits, a story which appears in Richard Branson's biography. Not only did Branson revel in Arnold's mistake, he also got his name wrong.

Arnold had great passion for the station and for music, and was enormously supportive of us, particularly in our first few weeks on air while we struggled to find our feet. If a new album or single landed on his desk during our show, he'd run in and make us play it straight away. Enthusiasm like that was infectious.

He was legendary for his love of a long lunch at a record company's expense. He took me out to lunch at the Hellenic Club in our first year and we ate slow-cooked lamb and drank horrible retsina that I think they'd actually used to kill the animal we'd just eaten. He kindly offered to pay and when the bill arrived he threw down his Bankcard. Even though this was 1999, I swear I hadn't seen a Bankcard used by anyone since Nan bought me a pair of desert boots in the mid '80s. It may have been that long since Arnold had paid for a lunch.

At the music meetings, Arnold would pop on a song without telling us the name of the artist or title, so we would listen 'without prejudice' George Michael-style. Sometimes the little charade was useless; it is rather difficult after all to disguise a new U2 song. There would often be heated arguments about songs or artists, with Arnold often losing to the power of the majority. I always admired the passion of fellow presenters Robbie Buck and Richard Kingsmill, who always fought the good fight for Australian bands.

Not only would we decide whether songs would be played on air, we'd decide how often they'd be played in rotation. The most popular was played up to four times a day. At the end of the meeting there would also be a review of all the current playlist and we'd determine which songs 'sounded great on air' and would be played more and which had been played enough and were to be rested.

I'm sure there are many people who, despite a firm belief in democracy, wonder how the musical careers of so many artists ended up being partially in the hands of a couple of fuckwits like Merrick and Rosso.

Sometimes albums would land on your desk and you'd play a track before they went to the music meeting. This was the case for us with the first Coldplay record, *Parachutes*. I listened to it and straight away knew we had to play 'Yellow' on the show that day and we did.

Triple J was extremely important to record companies, particularly in the '90s. The commercial stations would listen closely to what was played and jump on board with a song if it had gained momentum. Certain singles wouldn't get a run on the narrow playlists of commercial radio unless they had had a run on the youth station. Scottish band Travis can thank Francis Leach for their success in Australia. Arnold hated their single 'Why Does It Always Rain On Me?' and commercial radio wouldn't touch it, despite it being a number one single in the UK. Francis persisted with playing it on his show and the song gained momentum and was a hit here too. With results like these, record companies would push extremely hard to gain airplay in order to break some artists with some interesting results.

There were some raised eyebrows—and raised voices too—around the station when the very commercial-sounding Melbourne pop rock outfit Taxi Ride got their bubblegum pop single 'Get Set' on the radio without it going to the music meeting. I think it must have been the Triple J playlist fairy who managed to get that one coming out the speakers.

Some songs are growers and you can't tell instantly what they will sound like on the radio, so we would often put them aside and take another listen the next week. One such song was the second single for Victorian band Killing Heidi. This talented brother and sister team had been discovered by Triple J as part of its unsigned band competition Unearthed. Still teenagers, Ella and Jesse had had enormous success with their first single 'Weir' and they'd certainly charmed us when they'd come in and played it live for us and then asked us for our autographs.

When their next single, 'Mascara', came out, however, it was put on ice for a week. That night we went off to a music industry function where Merrick, who'd had a couple of beers, bumped into Jesse coming out of the dunnies and told him that despite the fact that we loved 'Weir', the new single was not going to cut it and he was sorry that he had to let him down gently. The next week, with fresh ears everyone loved the song, it was put on high rotation, then commercial radio picked it up and it went to Number 1 on the charts.

The boardroom wasn't just for music meetings; it also had one of the few phones on which you could make international calls. Most nights when we walked out the door at around 6.30, a staff member could be found with his feet on the boardroom table happily chatting away to his family overseas.

I've been told many times, 'Don't meet your heroes because you're bound to be disappointed'. As my first job in the media, the gig at Triple J showed me that you had to take the good with the bad. Just before we moved to Sydney to start the new show, I picked up a gig asking Tim Rogers some questions for a 'that was the year that was' kind of MTV documentary. I was, and still am, a massive You Am I fan and I wasn't alone when it came to man crushes on the charismatic lead singer. In 1993 I'd been at a barbecue in Collingwood when the whole backyard uprooted and moved to the Punters Club in Fitzroy to catch one of the band's early Melbourne shows.

I met Tim at a warehouse in Richmond with one page of generic questions. The interview was only supposed to last ten minutes maximum. An hour later, it finally came to an end when the cameraman ran out of tape and the sound guy's arm had almost fallen off from holding the boom mike above us as I'd asked Timmy every question I could think of and more. A great musician and a great bloke, who has a crooked smile I never tire of seeing.

Our first week of the Drive Show coincided with the Big Day Out tour, so we were definitely thrown in the deep end with the interviews that were scheduled. On our second day we had Norman Cook aka Fatboy Slim live on the show and, despite our nerves, he was a great chat and things were going well until he completely froze and stopped talking because he thought he saw an ex-girlfriend in the studio next door. Thankfully, he relaxed when he realised it was just Richard Kingsmill in a rather feminine white shirt.

Richard, who hosted the Australian Music Show, the New Music Show and the J Files, was always on the wrong end of our practical jokes. Inspired by the rather weird German metal act Rammstein that we were playing on air, Merrick took to only talking to Richard in a German accent, which drove Kingsmill mad. He'd end up hiding in his office while Merrick chased him down the hallway screaming 'Ja Richard, what da you think of da new Powderfinger record. It's wunderbar, ja?'

Because he played a lot of unsigned music on the Australian Music Show, Richard would come in to work and sift through loads of messages from up-and-coming bands looking for airplay. Being the marvellously conscientious broadcaster he is, he would always endeavour to call everyone back. Taking advantage of his generous nature, I'd leave longwinded messages as the brain-dead lead singer of a death metal band from Hobart, humming the tunes to non-existent songs and always leaving my mobile number for Richard to call. He must have called me on at least ten different occasions looking for an assortment of fictional pot-smoking musicians and as soon as I answered the phone his response was always the same: 'Tim Ross, you fucking idiot.' Slam, phone down.

I think I realised that I was becoming obsessed when I started taping Bon Jovi album tracks onto cassettes, pretending they were demo tracks from a new band from Adelaide and hoping Richard would play them on air.

Also in that first week we interviewed James Dean Bradfield the lead singer of the Manic Street Preachers. This Welsh outfit was a band I knew little about so I'd relied pretty heavily on Jen Oldershaw, our producer, for help. The main story she knew about the band was that the guitarist, Richey Edwards, had disappeared, presumed dead, in 1995. We thought it was a pretty dark topic to talk about, particularly for a couple of comedians in their first week of a national radio show. However, she was adamant that the audience would be interested and she singled me out to pursue the line of questioning.

The budding thespian.
Stills from 'White
With Wire Wheels'.
La Trobe University
Drama Studio, 1995.

Funny 'dag rock' gains cult st

THEY call it "Dag Rock". Look out — it is very catchy and very funny.

What else can you say about a band such as Black Rose, whose members describe themselves as "Chiko Roll-munching, Bali-singlet-stretching, gag-oriented, Passiona-skulling legends"?

After winning La Trobe University's Battle Of The Bands contest some years ago, the band earned a cult following due to songs such as *I Drive A Holden (My One's A Brown One)*, *We're Not From Seattle But We Still Wear Flannel*, *All I Want Is My Photo In Beat*, *Skeg Surfing In East Doncaster* and *Bryon Bay*.

Earlier this year Black Rose was a Melbourne Comedy Festival surprise hit, described by Cameron Adams in *Beat* magazine as "like TISM, but very, very good". Its influences include The Uncanny X-Men and the David Reyne-Tracey Mann ABC music series, *Sweet and Sour*.

Black Rose will perform in the Melbourne Fringe Festival at The Public Bar, North Melbourne on October 3, 10 and 17.

☐ ☐ ☐

THE Continental Cafe in Prahran continues its great Tuesday night residency series, this month featuring Maurice Frawley and The Working Class Ringoes.

Following sessions by Spencer Jones and Dave Last, The Conti-

Don't be fooled by the name. Black Rose are the funniest Oz rock band since Roxus. They're kind a like TISM but really, really good. "I don't think there is anyone that can compare to us," boasts Tim. "That sounds a bit conceited. We hark back to those Barnsey/Farnsey days. We like to think of ourselves as a Faberge-tightening, Adidas-wearing, Bali-singleted type of band. Gag oriented Oz rock."

Black Rose, Melbourne's funniest band, explodes into the Comedy Festival with a gag infested rock and roll extravaganza entitled *Putting The Fab Back Into Faberge.*

In'Press Magazine 12th April 1995

Local heroes: Blending rock with humor has made Black Rose a sensation.

Comedy

Tim Ross, Juck Sims and Anthony Snooks can't play jazz, but they do promise Lively and Provocative Conversation. No doubt Australia Day will pop up as a topic for the comedy trio to banter, babble and squabble about. The boys are holding court at the Bluestone Stage, off the William Street entrance to the Flagstaff Gardens, from 3 to 6pm today. Talk is not only cheap: it's free, and food and drink is available. Not that it rains in Melbourne during January, but if it does, scamper up to the Public Bar, on Victoria and Elizabeth, where the conversation, controversy and all that jazz will continue.

THE AGE ENTERTAINMENT GUIDE

2 26 JANUARY 1996

EG

Black Rose is the fringe act most suited to a pub, and its gig at The Public Bar is hugely amusing. An original parody band a la Spinal Tap, Black Rose takes off the suburban band scene something rotten — a vision in skin-

■ **FIONA SCOTT-NORMAN**

THE BULLETIN, OCTOBER 24, 1995

tight stretch denim jeans and singlets, pumping out original songs such as *Cock Rock* and *(Why Don't You Fuck Off Back To) Byron Bay*. The inter-song badinage is humorous and the characters are tacky, excessive and yet grounded in reality ... a treat.

**BLACK ROSE
(Rochester Castle Hotel)**

There are 120 acts on during this year' Melbourne International Comedy Festiva I've managed to sample a few - som hilarious, some dreadful but none quite lik Black Rose.

Black Rose have brought their 'Puttin The Fab Back Into Faberge Tour' to th Rochester Castle for a limited season toutin their rock extravaganza as being bigger tha Gavin Woods 3XY Windcheater, now that got to be pretty bloody big. Clad in fashion that immediately reminded me, sadly, of m youth in the outer suburbs of Melbourne complete with stretch jeans, bad hairdo (albeit wigs in this case - I hope!) Black Rose hit the stage with a frantic version of the ol classic Don't Wait To Be Told, You Nee Palmolive Gold. By half way through I Driv A Holden (My One's a Brown One), I wa tempted to go to the bar and ask if they ha any Brandivino, Stones, or Boronia Marsal

This was a very, very funny show wit some absolutely classic moments that even am at a loss to describe in a way that woul do them justice. Still I have chuckled t myself many times since that night ove Chevron Rockdog and Fast Times at Blac Rose High. This band has to be seen to b believed, it's a real location thing, you jus had to be there. It's a cleverly thought ou and very well executed satire of the good ol Oz pub band, and tragic though it may seen there are still some of these bands out ther doing the same thing, but taking themselve very seriously. Black Rose still have couple more weeks at the Rochester Cast and I can't recommend them highly enoug But be warned, get those face muscles i training because you'll be smiling overtim

★ L.B. Berminghat

"We've just got back from Bowral," says Tim, the unmistakable voice of Black Rose, a new Melbourne band who are single-handedly reviving Oz rock. "We were up to donate a song we'd written for the Tin Lids new album. It's called *My Old Man's A Piss Head*. But they said we were too late, but they'll keep it in mind next time."

BEAT

Reviews: we had a few . . . some were even good.

Black Rose: "We are a tribute to rock and roll."

ARTS

AGE, 4/10/95.
INTERVIEW

THE BOYS from rock and roll or die band Black Rose claim to have taught The Sharons everything they know about *ruk and rull*. The five bewigged (an essential for cabaret rock and roll) musicians, who moonlight with slightly more serious bands, belt out original music that is derivative of '80s Oz hard rock circa Brian Mannix of the Uncanny X Men, Swanee, Bon Scott and maybe Noiseworks. The boys emphasise they are not a tribute to any one

band. "We are a tribute to rock and roll."

Hursto (drums), Rosso (vocals and gags), Lordo (tambourine), Chops (guitar) and Killer (bass) certainly live the lifestyle. The long pitch-black hallway leads to the loungeroom, messy with old stuffed chairs, itchy things, overflowing ashtrays, foam couches, smoke-discolored walls, plastered with posters of rock heroes and carpet that moves. This was the place for an interview. Splayed around a connecting room are at least 10 loads of dirty washing. It is the classic rock and roll dwelling.

"We are the band that think we really made it and still are the biggest band in the world. But never quite did. Egos are running rampant. We've 'played with' Barnesy and Farnsey and we're 'mates' with Molly Meldrum." Next year they will host a stage show based on *Countdown* for the Comedy Festival.

Black Rose began as a joke and

ended up in the finals of the National Campus Battle of the Bands. Songs such as *I Drive a Holden, F... Off Back to Byron Bay, Chevron Rock Dog* and *We're Not From Seattle But We Still Wear Flannel* reeked of success. And they haven't looked back. After two years they are revered by the inner-city pub dwellers who not only laugh but appreciate the music and drink lots of beer (atmosphere).

"We don't spend months writing songs but (our musicianship) must come through. If it's not happening in five or 10 minutes we don't worry about it," they say. "We run with all the cliches. Our song *CockRock* is a classic AC/DC, Rolling Stones approach."

Well if that isn't a recommendation, what is?

Girls, Guitars and Big Fast Cars is playing The Prince of Wales Hotel, St Kilda, at 9pm from 16 October until 1 November. Black Rose are playing The Public bar 16, 23 and 30 October.

ROSSO GOES SOLO AGAIN

OzRock superspunk frontman Rosso dons the robe and ditches the boys from his band Black Rose for a solo session at the Espy once again. Catch the Chiko Roll munching little bloke on Sunday arvo August 7 as he ploughs through the best and worst of the Black Rose gags.

Frolicking on the Fringe

HERALD-SUN 10/10/95

REVIEW
comedy

Make-up

Where: Rochester Castle Hotel, Johnston St, Fitzroy

Black Rose

Where: Public Bar, Victoria St, North Melbourne

By FIONA SCOTT-NORMAN

Later, I recommend chugging along to the Public Bar to see Black Rose, a tongue-in-cheek rock band on much the same level as Spinal Tap, resembling a low-rent Ted Mulry Gang.

Black Rose is the epitome of every dreadful suburban band, with skin-tight stretch denims, vicious testicle separation, tight singlets and love handles.

Their song list includes such classics as *Chevron Rockdog, Tell The Chicks* and *Byron Bay.*

Black Rose is a big cack and a must for anyone who has been part of the band scene.

Rose on the nose: *Black Rose churns out classic comedy hits.*

BEAT ● ———————▶ Another hiccup is that singer Rosso is currently traipsing around the stand up circuit, and brings his Oz Rockin' World Of Comedy to the Rochester Castle on Wednesday October 19. Guests include Billsy, Juck, Mud, Mullet, Snooksy, Cole Trickle, Jed and a cameo appearance from Jazzin' Walter Klondike and the Coaches Award. $2 entry.

Publicity shot for the Big League Tour with Heavy Denver, 1994.

Black Rose, on stage, Rochester Castle Hotel Fitzroy, 1994.

Megsy and Bulldog at another house party.
Somebody forgot to tell Bulldog that we cancelled the Dr Seuss theme.

Not a dry eye in the house. Carpsy's final show, Public Bar, North Melbourne, 1996.
Left to right: Lordo, Killer, Rosso, Hursto, Carpsy.

Left to right: Killer,
Carpsy, Rosso, Hursto,
Lordo.

Photo shoot for our
debut EP, 'Fast Times at
Black Rose High'.

Black Rose, feeling
Thursday in our lounge
room in Chapman St,
North Melbourne, 1996.
Don't bother about
taking the bong out of
the shot, lads.

Employee of the month, ABC, 2000

Publicity shot from 'Pissheads From Outer Space'. Merrick Watts and Tim Ross. We were a classy act from day one.

Somebody had to protect our troops from the amateur photographer. East Timor, 2000

Dad always wanted to go to
Easter Island, so we went
in 2005.

I was really uncomfortable and didn't have any idea of what to specifically ask him. Jen thought that Richey had apparently turned up so perhaps I could just ask James about that.

James came into the studio and before the mikes came on, Jen asked him if he was comfortable about questions about Richey. This put him on the back foot and he raised his finger and said, 'Just one'. After a few generic questions about the Big Day Out, I could feel Jen's eyes burning into the back of my head, willing me to ask the question which went like this: 'James, Richey your guitarist strangely disappeared in 1995 but he's turned up, yes?'

'No.'

On saying that, he just looked down at the floor because the reason Richey hadn't turned up was because he was, unfortunately, dead. Thanks for that, Jen.

I'd been a big fan of New York blues punk outfit Jon Spencer Blues Explosion and had pushed pretty hard to have them on the show even though the station seldom played them. I came into work with a couple of their albums for them to sign. Unfortunately, they were rude and rather than answer questions Spencer simply rambled on like a gospel preacher with a high-pitched scream of

'I'm Jon Spencer from the Blues Explosion from New York City!' The interview never made it to air and I never asked him to sign my CDs.

Ben Folds, a talented and funny man, proved to be a difficult fish during a promotion where we gave away his piano to the listener who wrote the best song about us in the style of Ben Folds Five. We had some incredibly clever entries and Ben was in the studio to sign the piano (it wasn't actually his, but the same type that he played) and be there to talk to the winner when we called them. He was chatty and fine until the microphones came on, after which he barely spoke and when I asked him to play something on the piano he just hit the keys with a karate chop like a four-year-old child. Something was going on behind the scenes.

Other times, he's been a wonderful interview and happily did a prank call for us once, calling a number from an ad in the street press where someone was looking for a keyboard player for a covers band. During the call, he was asked the perfect question: 'Have you had much experience?' 'Yes, I'm Ben Folds and I've toured the world!'

Maynard from Tool made for an interesting interview when touring with his side project A Perfect Circle.

He blankly ignored questions, leaving his embarrassed guitarist to answer them for him. After four excruciatingly painful minutes we wrapped up the interview and were then press ganged into standing next to him for a photo for the website. He refused to pose unless he was wearing a ridiculous long black wig. This apparently differentiated him from his Tool persona. No prizes for guessing the inspiration for the band name.

Most guests were a complete joy to interview. The late Joe Strummer from The Clash was an absolute gentleman, who just loved being in Australia with his band the Mescaleros. I asked him about the contentious issue of playing songs from The Clash in his Big Day Out set and he answered simply and beautifully: 'Those songs are part of life, they're as much my songs as anyone else's and I have a right to play them, so I will.' It was a real pleasure to interview him and I was saddened by his death a few years ago.

Robbie Williams was the first guest who was actually surprised by us! His solo career was slow to kick off in Australia and he was a surprise choice as a guest on the show. It was the novelty of his status as a former boyband member as much as his duet with Kylie that got him in the studio in front of the microphone.

I must admit I was taken aback by how handsome the bloke was; he had star quality that is actually seldom seen. Obviously he was a superstar in the UK and people got incredibly nervous around him but he could not believe how we were in the studio. 'You guys are incredible. I've done a million interviews and people are always scatty and hyper but you guys are just so laidback it's awesome.'

Neither of us had the heart to tell him we were simply unprofessional.

Six years later I bumped into him in a department store in LA and he was kind enough to pretend to remember our interview. When he walked off I started chatting to a sales attendant and told her I'd just been talking to Robbie Williams. He'd walked out with half a dozen shopping bags and I wondered out loud what he'd bought and suddenly she started checking out his account on the computer.

She found it and I went behind the counter to have a look. She'd misheard me and thought that I'd said Robin Williams and there I was looking at the famous comedian's account, complete with his home address and phone number. Who would have thought the man who was Mork from Ork would have bought a pair of Apple Bottom Jeans?

During our two years, we had a great line-up of regulars who popped in to shoot the shit. Fellow comedian Peter Helliar presented a very successful segment 'Peter Helliar PI' where we'd give him a challenge to track down famous people who had dropped off the radar. Pete conveniently left Jen and me to do most of the groundwork to track people down and I remember a late-night call to the ornithological society in London that successfully got me the home number of Bill Oddie from *The Goodies* (Bill is a mad birdwatcher apparently) and giving him a call. It was a kooky experience to call someone I'd grown up watching on TV and catch him while he was cooking himself a kipper for breakfast. A terrific bloke, he was more than happy to be 'found' by Pete.

His co-star Tim Brooke-Taylor came on the show once and got rather upset when I tried on his trademark Union Jack waistcoat for a photo opportunity. I was a little chubby at the time so perhaps his concerns were warranted.

Pete's standout piece was when we gave him a challenge to write a musical about former Young Talent Timer Beven Adinsall. Teaming up with Gatesy from the musical comedy trio Tripod, their song, in which they cleverly substituted 'Beven' for 'Heaven' in well-known songs like 'Tears from Heaven', was a smash.

When we invited the boys on to perform it during a live show we were doing at the HiFi Bar and Ballroom in Melbourne it brought the house down, particularly when we organised Beven to join them on stage for the final stanza.

Tony Squires started off being our sports guy and he tried to leave us a couple of times because he was busy with his terrific TV sports show *The Fat*. He finally dragged himself away from us and we ended up getting Matty White, who was then a sports presenter at Channel 10. He happily popped in once a week on a Friday and didn't think much of it until he was doing a live cross for Ten News from the Bathurst 1000 and hundreds of pissed dudes starting singing the intro jingle that we'd written for his segment 'Matty White, Matty White wears his jockstrap real tight, Matty White'.

Triple J legend Robbie Buck was always popping his head in on the show and had the nation grooving and shaking with his funk and disco classics that he played every Friday afternoon. Rolling in wearing a western shirt and quite often carrying an open stubby he provided the vibe for our show and was awesome playing the nerd Joey in our weekly serial 'Choice Bro Tafe'. The South African Headmaster, Hansie, who couldn't use a computer and always walked around in a black leather jacket carrying a printout of emails with replies written in pencil, was based on our general manager Ed Breslin. Whatever he said to us that week was always put in the script, even if it didn't make sense. I mean what South African headmaster worth his salt would mention that 'an interview with Jennifer Byrne went for three minutes too long'. By the end I think Hansie used to write on butchers' paper with crayons. Ed never realised Hansie was based on him.

Another regular was Tom the Chippy from Manly. A caller with a great sense of humour, he also happened to be a 'total hunk' and went on to become a star on Channel 7 and is also a great mate.

I loved the unpredictability of the show, especially one afternoon when we managed to take the radio station off air. We were broadcasting from the Radio National studios downstairs while the Triple J studios were being renovated when I playfully dared Merrick to push a big red button on the studio wall marked 'Do Not Push'. What followed was the audience hearing the rather refined Jen Oldershaw as they'd never heard her before. This is the transcript of what went to air:

Rosso: Go on have a go!

Merrick: I'll shut it off!

Rosso: 1 ... 2 ... 3

Clicking sound

Oldershaw: OHHHHHH!

Merrick: Did I shut down the radio station?

Oldershaw: OHHHH ... What the hell did you just do?

Merrick: He just told me to shut it off.

Oldershaw: You just fucking ...

Merrick: I just shut off the radio station.

Oldershaw: You're a fucking idiot!

Merrick laughs nervously

Merrick: He told me to do it.

Rosso: Can we play a track?

Oldershaw: The mikes are still on.

At that stage we realised that when Merrick had pushed the red button it had frozen the computer system that controlled the radio panel but it had left the microphones on and everything we'd said had gone to air. As Jen stormed out of the studio leaving Mez and me giggling, the back-up tape thankfully kicked in, playing the Foo Fighters while the techs came and sorted everything out.

It must have been a strange thing to hear on the radio on your way home from work.

Our listeners often gave us our best content and came along for the ride with every stupid idea we had. When I read veteran talkback king John Laws's *Sunday Telegraph* column where he complained about the price of lobster at Catalina, an expensive fine diner he frequented, I couldn't believe it. Here was a bloke who had a golden microphone, one of the richest men in showbiz, having a whinge about the price of a crustacean. Concerned for the little Aussie battler, we rallied concerned citizens to help him out and send him a crabstick in the mail so he could have a taste of the seafood he so badly craved. After giving out the address for his station 2UE on air, his office was bombarded with envelopes and postpacks containing crabsticks. A couple of generous souls even threw in a couple of dim sims for good measure. John and the folk at 2UE took the joke well until one over-zealous listener in Canberra couriered him a complete fisherman's platter after it had been left out in the sun for a couple of days!

Our two biggest segments, Tightarse Tuesday and Hello Australia, relied almost exclusively on listeners' stories. Tightarse Tuesday was based on the colloquial term that everyone used for half-priced Tuesdays at the cinema. On Tuesdays, we'd share people's stories about tightarse friends and relatives, and there never seemed to be any shortage. There was a mum who kept fingernail and toenail clippings and put them in old stockings to make a handy kitchen scourer and an uncle who walked around McDonald's asking people to give him the pickles they didn't want from their burgers, then he'd take them home and put them in a jar of vinegar.

My favourite would have to be the girl whose Nanna had remarried a man whose first wife had died two years before. One day she asked whether she could get some new clothes; the husband replied, 'Why do you need new clothes? You can just wear my dead wife's!'

Hello Australia was a celebration of the silly and often dumb things that we do as Australians. Stories like the dad who once a month drove down to Phillip Island to mow the block of land on which one day they were going to build the family a holiday house. Then one day he turned up and half a house had been built there. Incensed that someone had been building on his land, he checked the paperwork and seemed that he'd been mowing the wrong block of land for fifteen years. Theirs was the one next door.

Mowing was a familiar theme. Another dad grabbed a mower from the nature strip on his street, where it had been put out for council clean-up. It wasn't until there was a knock on the door fifteen minutes later and he was confronted by the mower's angry owner that he realised that the mower hadn't been left out for council clean-up at all but that it had run out of petrol and his neighbour had left it there while he went to get a jerry can to fill it up.

I also loved the tale about a couple of teenage boys who lived on a farm and got their guns out for some target practice when their parents went out for the day. Setting up a series of cans and bottles against the wall of an old shed, they had a great old time and were careful to clean up the mess before their folks got home.

As a result they were surprised to find their old man screaming at them for using the guns without his permission. What they didn't realise was that their dad had parked the Holden Statesman in the shed, directly behind where they'd been firing and they'd shot the shit out of his brand new car.

People came out in droves for our 'Love Bus Tours' when we grabbed an ABC broadcast van and took the show to the people. On the first tour we started in Newcastle with the boys from Silverchair, and then packed up and moved on, doing the show the next day from the uni in Armidale, then Byron Bay, Toowoomba, and finishing on the Friday in Brisbane with over 3000 people cramming into the Queen Street Mall to watch the show. It really was like being in a fishbowl and I can remember being extremely self-conscious as people found out firsthand what happens on radio when the songs are playing ... fuck all really.

The Love Bus really captured people's imagination and it was a fantastic way for us to meet many of the people who listened everyday. The tours were incredibly difficult things to put together and we did them all on a tiny budget, with people sharing crappy motel rooms and Jen Oldershaw and Nic Salisbury working tirelessly behind the scenes to get a show from a different town off the ground every day. When we arrived and plugged into the phone line it was always touch and go whether we were going to be on air. While Jen and Nic were smashing themselves to keep the show on the road, Merrick was at his hilariously insane best. After failing his truck driver's licence twice (he wanted to help out with the driving on tour) he had to be content to be navigator for our multi-talented sound engineer Cam McCauley.

Cam was a whiz with bands and had been You Am I's regular sound guy until he decided to have a change of pace and take on a 9 to 5ish lifestyle. When Cam and Mez were up front en route to Byron, a stone hit the front windscreen and caused a small chip. Merrick, once again mistaking himself for JFK, was convinced that we were under attack from an anti-ABC sniper in the bushes and ducked for cover.

Myf Warhurst, who was also a regular on the show, came with us on tours and the second one, which started in Bendigo, pulled into her hometown of Mildura after doing the second show in Swan Hill. All afternoon while we broadcast from Chaffy Park, opposite the Murray River, we kept banging on about the bad motel that the ABC had put us up in, which had the world's largest deck chair out the front. After the show, car after car pulled up at the motel with people streaming out carrying cases of beer and bourbon and Coke keen to have a drink with us. The problem was that we were having dinner at Myf's parents' place that night, and Mez, Myf and I were all staying the night there too. So while Ed and Nancee Warhurst entertained us in their stunning mudbrick home in the neighbouring town of Red Cliffs, Nic and Jen were entertaining fifty locals by the pool at the joint we'd nicknamed 'The Top Yourself Motel'. Even better, Cam, who the punters had mistaken for me (we did look slightly similar at the time), was holding court in the spa, calling everyone 'Tiger' and doing my shit stories.

The second and final Love Bus Tour finished up in Adelaide, with local heroes Super Jesus playing for us to a crowd of 2000 people on the lawns of Adelaide Uni. Hursto, who was having great success playing drums with Rocket Science had a gig in town that night, so it was a great way to finish the week up.

My favourite moment on that tour had happened the day before when we broadcast from the wonderful little South Australian town of Renmark. With the bus parked under a willow tree beside the Murray River, kids jumped off the pier into the cool murky brown water while we did the show. Hanging around was a gangly sixteen-year-old kid called James. An avid listener, he was very excited that we'd come to his town and he had a million questions about every aspect of our set-up, particularly the technical side. He had an engaging personality and we put him on air to tell us a bit about the town, and he was brilliant. After the show, Nic gave him some CDs and a Triple J T-shirt and he was stoked and he wandered off home. All packed up and heading out of town, we saw him up ahead walking along the highway. We stopped and offered to give him a lift and he excitedly jumped into the van and assured us he lived just up the road. The minutes passed and passed and we were a good 15 kilometres up the road by the time we hit his turn-off and headed down the narrow bitumen road. We pulled up at his small fibro house and he begged us to wait so he could bring out his mum to prove that he'd met us and that we'd given him a lift home. She came out in her dressing gown to say Hi and as we drove off we left a kid looking happier than anyone I'd ever seen in my life. He'd walked 20 kilometres to see us that day and would have walked the same back if we hadn't given him a lift.

That was the magical thing about Triple J for me. People could be on a tractor in the middle of Western Australia, stuck in a traffic jam on Punt Road, Richmond, or wondering what they'd done to deserve being born in Wagga Wagga and still tune in.

We used to get letters from international backpackers who listened to our show as they travelled all over the country. Somehow, over time, they understood what we were rabbiting on about and really enjoyed it. Our audience was amazing.

I bumped into Richie from Tumbleweed one time and he told me that while he did a stint working at a cardboard box factory, he got really excited when we came on at 3pm because our show helped him through the pain of the last two hours of a shit job each day. It remains to this day one of the nicest compliments I have received in my life.

Towards the end of 2000, we were having the time of our lives on the show, the ratings were great, we'd successfully toured our new show, Solid Gold, across the country, and were about to release an album of highlights from the show and a book ... and then the bad men came with a cheque book.

On offer was a chance to head up the breakfast show of an as yet unnamed and brand-new commercial radio station, the first new FM radio station in Sydney in over twenty years. This certainly threw a spanner in the works.

I loved my job, I loved working at Triple J and I really felt at home there. I didn't want to leave. But after meeting them, Merrick was convinced. I wasn't. The conversations went round and round in circles as I weighed up the pros and cons and discussed it with my family and closest friends.

Ultimately though, the thrill of a new challenge and the chance to be at the start of something new won the day. I'd also be lying if I didn't say that the offer was really too good to refuse.

All of the negotiations were secret and it became impractical to let anyone know that we were leaving. So on our final day on air, just before 6pm I went to say, 'We'll see you next year' but stopped at 'We'll see you ...' As the familiar Triple J news theme played, I put down my headphones and cried.

13
Oops, I did it again ... and again

In 2004, in between series of *Unplanned*, a TV show
Merrick and I were doing for the Nine network,
Hursto, Steve 'Pinko' Pinkerton from The Anyones and
I did four rock shows at the Newtown RSL. It featured
a bit of stand-up, a few choice covers, the odd bawdy
original, and some audience participation in the form of
a singing competition. With the lure of a bottle of red,

I managed to get the then *Australian Idol* judge Dicko to record a few judges' comments that I played off my sampler on stage after each contestant had sung a few bars of their favourite song. Needless to say the recorded comment that always brought the house down was Dicko's 'You useless no-talent cunt!' Classy stuff indeed!

The show managed to sell a few tickets so in a typical fit of responsibility we used the proceeds to top up Hursto's super ... no, I do believe we booked three tickets to New York. Unfortunately Pinko had a job and a family to look after, so Willow, our stage manager, mate and occasional bass player, picked up the slack.

Willow, like Hursto, has never been shy of a good time and hats should always go off to a man who once, having a special moment on the E, called every member of his family and told them how much he loved them for half an hour. The original family guy.

I had decided to pick up any available interviews for the radio show while I was there, and Channel 10 had organised a set visit to *Law and Order: Criminal Intent* so I could interview the stars.

I did some vigorous research the night before by going out to a bar called Arlene's Grocery on the Lower East Side and getting totally poleaxed. Every Monday night to a full house, they stage Rock 'n' Roll Karaoke with a full live band. Rather than your normal staple of Whitney Houston, Mariah Carey, and the songs from *Grease*, these guys have the likes of Mötley Crüe, Queen, Journey and Van Halen on the menu. Hursto and I hit the stage early and punched out a spirited version of Kiss's 'I Was Made for Loving You' only to be trumped by Willow doing 'You Shook Me All Night Long' with such gusto that the crowd carried him off stage.

Bathing in our own amateur awesomeness, the night was a late one.

The next morning we trudged off to the Meatpacking District to visit the set, which was housed in a converted warehouse. Hursto wisely refused to come so I guilted a still-drunk Willow into coming along to keep me company.

We arrived at 10am sharp and were given a quick tour of the costume department and then we were ushered into the captain's office where we were to wait for the captain himself, actor Jamey Sheridan, to join us. Leaving a couple of idiots alone on the set of an internationally famous television series is never a good idea; we quickly made ourselves at home by adding our own names and the name of Gary Woodencock to the chalkboard duty roster positioned behind the desk.

Jamey came in with a big smile and a pair of jeans hoisted up to his tits and was a very cool chat. Even when I was challenging him with such hard-hitting questions as, 'When it comes to the crunch, who would you rather be Starsky or Hutch?' and, 'Non-ballistic weapon of choice: Tazer or Mace?' Incidentally, he chose Starsky and Mace.

After ten of the best with Jamey, I got to talk to the beautiful Katherine Erbe, who was professional and rather sexy. She was also the first to notice that I had half of last night's cheeseburger still stuck in my beard but despite this she still happily chatted for ten minutes before I was ushered into the leading man's dressing-room. Vincent D'Onofrio is a 190-centimetre method actor and a fairly intense sort of dude. I'd interviewed him once before in Sydney and, of course, when I shook hands with him I reminded him of it and he didn't even feign any recall of the moment. He sat on his black leather couch with a Gibson semi-acoustic guitar on his lap really unable to comprehend why exactly he was chatting to me. Not that he was impolite but just imagine the look on your own face if one day your boss said to you, 'Hey, I'd like to introduce you to Solomon, he's over from Samoa and he'd like to watch you send some emails for ten minutes if that's okay?' and you'll get the idea of how Vincent felt about me.

With that interview in the can it was time for a speedy departure but the publicist insisted that we wait around to interview Courtney B Vance. Now Courtney had had a little moment with the producers because apparently he wasn't quite in the mood to be interviewed, but he also didn't want to miss out on the publicity, so because politically we had to interview all four major cast members we had to hang around to wait for him to 'feel the vibe'.

An hour later, he was ready for his five-minute chat. Now in my defence I have to say I wasn't at my best by this stage and the hangover was really starting to knock me around. I must also admit that I hadn't watched this particular offshoot of the *Law and Order* franchise as much as the others. So after a bumbling question about whether he liked the food on set I showed off why I'm not exactly Michael Parkinson when I offered the most clichéd question I could have possibly asked: 'Do you find when you walk down the street people mistake you for a police officer in real life?' To which he curtly replied, 'No, because I play an attorney'. I have never felt like such a dickhead in my life; not only did I not know anything about his character but I had no more questions up my sleeve. I was done. Everyone in the room was looking at me like I had just backed over the Wiggles in a truck and then taken Jeff's head off with a spade, so I just thanked him for his time and we packed up and walked off. The interview consisted of two questions and went for just over fifty seconds, and I can officially say that Courtney B Vance hates my guts.

There are certain things you cannot say without sounding like a complete wanker. Statements like, 'I don't go to Byron anymore—it's so 2005' or, 'If I'm in Paris, I only speak French' and, 'I've just been invited to a brunch at Cate Blanchett's house to meet Steven Soderbergh'.

The last one, I've actually said. It was a particularly surreal moment. Steven Soderbergh is an Academy Award-winning director whose films include *Erin Brockovich*, *Traffic*, *Oceans 11* and *The Informant*. Cate Blanchett and her husband Andrew Upton had invited him to direct/create a play for the Sydney Theatre Company of which they are artistic directors. They wanted him to meet creative people in Sydney and because one of the projects he had in mind was a comedy, they kindly asked Merrick and me to come along, shoot the breeze and see what turned up.

When we arrived it was a veritable who's who of Australian actors including Hugo Weaving, Joel

Edgerton, Sasha Horler, Rhys Muldoon, Justine Clark and, well … us.

It was an extremely friendly gathering and I happily tucked into the delicious croissants. Cate Blanchett would have to be one of the nicest, most down-to-earth people you could ever meet and she made a special effort to introduce Steven to us and explain our background, and then left us to chat while she sorted some coffee for new arrivals. Steven started telling us they had three projects that they were thinking about, and the previous night at dinner they had decided on dramatising a true story about the tragic murder of a toddler in Florida. Obviously not a funny story and Stevo wasn't going to need our comic stylings for this project. Now I've seen most of his films but the Margaret Pomeranz within wasn't busting out on this particular day as we started talking to him about his flight home that afternoon and the ins and outs of air travel within America.

We might as well have just asked about his favourite colour and whether he'd managed to see a koala while he was in Australia. The real low point came when the topic of LA airport came up. I thought I'd dazzle him with a story of bumping into actor Martin Sheen at the airport and getting a photo with him, and how Martin had told us that when he was doing *The West Wing* he'd got a letter from the Premier of Queensland Mike Brady, and I'd told him that Mike Brady was the dad in *The Brady Bunch* and that Mike Beattie was the then Queensland premier! How funny! Thoroughly unimpressing him with this amazing anecdote, I then said, 'And another time I saw Gene Simmons from Kiss at the airport. Do you know him?' Time slowed down for a second as I realised I had just asked an Academy Award winner the world's dumbest question. He stared at me with this incredulous look and simply said, 'No, but I've heard of him'. Then he politely excused himself and went to talk to Hugo Weaving.

STU

FF

Reality shows

Cracking the perfect television format is the fast track to riches. For every *Big Brother* or *Survivor* there's a *Celebrity Dog School* or *Pirate Master*. The trick is to think outside the square by looking directly at the square. Confused? Let me inspire you with a few of my TV ideas that are currently in development.

Prostitute roadshow

A more focused show than *Antiques Roadshow*, members of the public are encouraged to bring old photos of members of their family who were prostitutes in the late nineteenth- and early- to mid-twentieth century. Our panel of experts examines the snaps and then determines how much your ancestor would have charged by the hour in today's money.

Edelston wedding break

Each week a blonde contestant marries controversial doctor Geoffrey Edelston. They then have a week to get out of the marriage with more than half of his assets. To help them they have relevant sections of the *Family Law Act 1975* tattooed to their back to help them take him to the cleaners.

Master scientist

Some of the country's best amateur scientists battle it out for a coveted position at the CSIRO. Marvel as they have to disable a ticking nuclear device with nothing but a screwdriver and a can of WD40 in the pressure test. Sigh with amazement as they create a hybrid vehicle out of 12-volt battery and the remains of Dolly, the world's first cloned sheep. Be on the edge of your seat as they work out which apple has been sprayed with the banned carcinogenic pesticide DDT in the taste test. Judges include Dr Karl Kruszelnicki, Dr Tim Flannery and Kyle Sandilands.

Ten years Aussier in ten days

Recently arrived boat people are taken through their paces and given a dynamic makeover to make them Aussies in record time. After listening to right-wing talkback radio for ten minutes to ascertain why they've done wrong, our contestants are fed Vegemite by IV drip, forced to watch the last four Ashes series on DVD, are taught how to swear by Rodney Rude, and learn how to wear a green and gold tracksuit. Judges include John Howard, Bindi Irwin and Kyle Sandilands.

The wax factor

Take fifteen girls in their late thirties who've let themselves go something shocking and then let some of Australia's most talented beauticians go to work on a selection of the nation's most unkempt vaginas. Categories include the Brazilian, the bikini, the high bikini and the Peter Russell Clark. Judges include Sonia Kruger, Sophie Monk and Kyle Sandilands.

John Farnham wants a wife

To celebrate his seventieth birthday and latest comeback tour, old Whispering Jack decides to become a Mormon and take on another wife. He goes on a series of dates with the hopefuls, impressing them with the same trick at dinner every time—throwing his microphone in the air and catching it. He chooses the one person who doesn't say, 'I've seen that before, Farnsie.'

Come die with me

Four people who have recently lost a family member plan what they believe is the perfect funeral. The other contestants attend the funeral and wake. At the end of the day they each rate the occasion out of ten. Whoever has the highest score gets the funeral paid for.

The health inspectors

Health inspectors visit restaurants and take-away outlets to check on their level of hygiene. Viewers vote via SMS to punish establishments that appear to be violating the relevant health codes. For the worst offenders the public decides whether their businesses should be closed down.

Surprise celebrity renovator

Famous people are tricked into renovating a house without realising they are doing it. In Episode 1, former *Australian Idol* Paulini thinks she is helping a friend dig a hole for a traditional Fijian lovo feast. After half a day digging a bigger hole than normal, host Richard Wilkins runs out and lets her know that there will be no hot coals or roasted pork and that she has actually dug a hole for the Wilson family's new in-ground pool. Gotcha!

Movie sequels

How good is going to the movies! At this stage I must apologise if you are reading this book in prison because you probably won't be going to IMAX for quite sometime—unless you're getting out soon, so then it's something for you to look forward to. But for the other jailbirds, I'm sorry. So for you I say: how good is going out to the yard to exercise? Unless of course you've been stabbed in the yard with a blunt screwdriver—then it's not so good.

Anyways, I do love going to the cinema but I don't like people who talk during films. Sometimes it can be slightly amusing though, like the time I went to see *Milk*, the Sean Penn film about the life of politician and gay rights activist Harvey Milk. In the first ten minutes of the film, it predictably features two men being intimate. An elderly gentleman in front of me, wearing a hearing aid, turned to his wife during this scene and said, less than subtly, 'Crikey, it's a bit poofy, isn't it?' Well spotted, I say.

The thing about movies is that the film companies love to make sequels because they make loads of cash. This is fantastic for movies like *Jaws*, *Star Wars*, *Back to the Future* and *Police Academy*, but too often some of your other favourite films don't get a second chance. How many times have you asked yourself, 'Why don't they make another *Rain Man*? Why don't they make another *Titanic*?' Well, because sometimes there's not another story in that film. But what if you combined two successful films to create one sequel? Not only would you combine the stories but you would also gain double the fans and spread the financial risks. Wake up, George Lucas, it's time to taste the future Beardy!

Here are some obvious examples.

Viva Las Avatar

I'm sure this movie has been in production in James Cameron's mind since 1968, but just in case, here's a storyline to get everyone in Hollywood excited.

After the Na'vis kicked the humans' butts, a computer virus caused by someone leaving a curling wand on back on Earth renders the humans' Avatar technology useless. Fortunately a young army recruit (played by the singing teacher from *Glee*) comes up with a brilliant low-tech solution that will once again allow infiltration of Pandora's indigenous Na'vi. Under the cover of darkness, the army choppers in four members of the world-famous Blue Man Group (fresh from another hit season at the MGM Grand in Vegas), who pretend to be their bogan cousins from the nearby planet Pandora Bracelet. Codenamed the Avartards, their combination of music, comedy, multimedia theatrics and multiple-helicopter gunships wins the day for the humans.

Rated G

Sliding Gallipoli

This sequel combining the two movies *Sliding Doors* and *Gallipoli* is bound to be a box-office smash. In the first half of the movie we see how different life would have been for actor Mark Lee if he had gone on to the level of Hollywood success of co-star Mel Gibson. In the second half, we see a different life for Gwyneth Paltrow. In this parallel universe she never marries Chris Martin but instead falls in love with Huey Lewis on the set of *Cruising*. They are then both transported back in time to 1915 and are shot in the chest by the Turks at Anzac Cove.

Rated PG

There's Nothing About Molly Ringwald

In this double sequel to *There's Something About Mary* and *Sixteen Candles*, Ben Stiller wakes up one day haunted by the cuteness of 1980s sensation Ringwald, and her performance in *Sixteen Candles*. Using Facebook, he tracks down Molly on her fiftieth birthday, gatecrashes the shindig at the Church of Scientology, and realises that his teen crush is a thing of the past. He then takes off his shirt to prove to us that he's still working out.

Rated M

Old School 2. Driving Miss Daisy

Frank the Tank (Will Ferrell) still finds himself unable to shake those partying ways of his frat house days. After an intervention by his family and a professional counsellor, it is decided that Frank should become a driver for an old lady called Miss Daisy to help him understand that there is more to life than partying. Reluctantly at first, Frank eventually develops an enduring and close friendship with Miss Daisy, which culminates in them sharing a keg of Budweiser and doing a nude run through the local mall.

Rated R

Xanasaw

After seven *Saw* films, it's time to squeeze
one more out of this horror/slash franchise by
combining it with the sequel to *Xanadu*. The plot
revolves around Jeff Lynne, singer of the 1970s
progressive rock band ELO, who wrote much of the
music for the original soundtrack of Xanadu.
Jeff is on holidays in Mexico when he discovers
the whereabouts of Olivia Newton John's missing
lover, Patrick McDermott. Patrick had, of course,
faked his own death to get away from Olivia,
who refused to stop singing songs from her last
successful movie. The arrival of the megabearded
Jeff in a tight pair of tennis shorts sends
McDermott into a maniacal rage and he hacks
Jeff's head off with a saw, only to watch it hit
the floor and 'Turn to Stone'.

Rated G

Jurassic Nemo Forrestinator

Take four of the biggest films of all time—
Jurassic Park, *Forrest Gump*, *Finding Nemo* and
Terminator—and create an animated masterpiece
that will take the world by storm. It is the
year 2096 and the world is a different place. A
cyborg warlord called Forrestinator walks from
the west to the east coast of the United States
looking for gumbo shrimps to power a machine that
not only plays an antique collectors' edition

of *Finding Nemo* on Blu-Ray, but can bring its central character to life. However, he finds Nemo to be rather annoying and pan fries the little fish with a lemony butter sauce. Not satisfied with the dish, he sends his butler John Connor back to the year 2006 to fetch a bottle of Marlborough Sauvignon Blanc to complement the meal.

Rated G

The Notebook Crashers

Owen Wilson and Vince Vaughn are back together again but this time instead of crashing weddings to meet chicks, they crash into the homes of people who are watching *The Notebook* and reveal the heartwarming twists in the plot to ruin the movie for them. Hilarious madcap antics!

Rated R

Risky Valkyrie

Tom Cruise, reprising his role as Joel in *Risky Business*, discovers that his neighbour, the new German Ambassador to the US, is a neo-Nazi. Preying on the ambassador's implied homosexuality, Joel lures him over to his house by seductively dancing in his underpants—and then runs him over with his dad's Porsche 928.

Rated PG

My Left Footloose

Kevin Bacon and Daniel Day-Lewis are together again for the very first time in this haunting story of two disabled brothers who find salvation in the power of dance while playing a simplified version of soccer in the dunnies of I Hop Diner in the Bible Belt of Middle America. Featuring an incredible soundtrack that includes a duet between Kenny Loggins and Ice T.

Rated PG

Look Who's Talking About Three Men and a Ghost Dancing Baby

Ted Danson, Steve Guttenberg and Tom Selleck find themselves looking after a baby that has the voice of Bruce Willis. If this isn't weird enough, the baby is actually Patrick Swayze reincarnated and despite not yet being two, he can dance like a thirty-five-year-old in extremely high-waisted jeans. The film also stars Whoopi Goldberg, who plays a meddling woman from child welfare, who chastises the three of them for allowing the boy to sleep on the floor of his room. Her line to them is the classic 'Nobody puts baby in a corner!'

Rated PG

Whacky radio ideas that never made it

Golden retriever or dad

The contestant is blindfolded and brought into the studio. She then has to pat something on the head and decide whether it's her dad or a golden retriever that she's patting. It sounds easy but there's a twist, the dog is wearing a wig!

Celebrity pop-offs

When visiting celebrities visit the station they are asked to kindly do a fluff into a specimen jar, which is then put aside. When the contestant comes in they have to open the jar and with the aid of smell and some simple clues guess the owner of the celebrity flatulence.

Summer of '69er

A brother and sister come in and a coin is tossed to see which one is to be blindfolded. They are then placed with someone, fully clothed, in a 69er position. Then by sniffing the person's jeans in front of them they have to work out whether it's their sibling or a complete stranger in order to win 50 bucks.

Eat your mother-in-law's weight in her undies

In order to win the honeymoon of a lifetime, the groom has to devour his mother-in-law's weight in her underwear. To make things easier the bog catchers in question are dished up in a moussaka cooked by George from *MasterChef*.

Smack or be smacked

In the ultimate Mother's Day competition, a random mum is faced with the ultimate dilemma. In order to win the chance to have a walk-on role in the next *Sex and the City* movie, she has two choices: either to smack her young child with an open hand in front of an officer from the Department of Community Services or inject heroin for the very first time. You choose mummy, Carrie's waiting to meet you!

War vet or animal vet

Fancy an all-expenses paid trip to LA and Disneyland? Well, you either choose to sleep with an insane Vietnam war veteran or put down a beloved pet in front of its owners.

Win a salary cap for your office

Why should professional footy players be the only ones to have the laws of free trade restricted by a salary cap? The first caller through when they hear the sound of an arse being put on a photocopier wins a salary cap for their office that will put a freeze on any wage rises. Your boss will love you for the money you've saved him but unfortunately he can't give you a raise due to the new restrictions.

The ultimate Michael Jackson prize

Are you the world's biggest Michael Jackson fan? Are you prepared to moonwalk the Great Wall of China to prove it? If so, one lucky winner will get to be buried alive next to Michael at his LA cemetery.

Robert Thomas size me

Imagine watching Matchbox 20 from your own private box at the Entertainment Centre. Then getting to meet the band after the show and joining them for a late-night meal of Chinese, with all the lemon chicken you can handle. Well, all you have to do is be prepared to undergo leg-shortening surgery to become the exact height of lead singer Rob Thomas.

Only joking

In order to win a family trip to the Gold Coast, a mum has to tell her ten-year-old, live on air, that she is adopted. After letting the kid cry for a couple of minutes, the whole whacky morning crew shouts out 'ONLY JOKING!'. The kid finally stops crying and after five sessions with a child psychologist gets to take the holiday of a lifetime with her mother.

PART

6

14

Here's a celebrity I prepared earlier

People often talk about the pitfalls of fame and how hard it is for celebrities to cope with the pressure of fame. What a load of bullshit! Celebrities get paid a fortune, are given many things for free and are treated like royalty. What's the downside? People want to talk to them in the street and occasionally the paparazzi want to take photos of them with their bits showing. I'm sure if they were faced with the prospect of a normal job and a mortgage they'd take the guy hiding in the bushes with the telephoto lens every time. I think living with a child with a disability would be tough—being a Hollywood celebrity not so much.

What has always amazed me about Hollywood actors is their insecurity. After years of interviewing them on the radio I have never been able to work out why they are not interested in talking about their old films. Obviously 1977 was a long time ago for Harrison Ford, but surely he'd have something to say about *Star Wars*? But actors may be terrified they will never reach those heights again. For us those films represent a great movie-going experience, to them they often signify the peak of their careers.

I was fascinated to meet Sylvester Stallone when he was out promoting the ridiculous *Rocky 5*. The *Rocky* and the *Rambo* series of films were massive when I was a kid, so I was intrigued to meet him. Let's face it, I would never have realised that you could get knives with a compass on the end if it hadn't been for John Rambo.

I knew Stallone was short but I wasn't ready for him to be *that* short as he strode into the room in a pair of platform sneakers, pleated jeans and a white shirt. He was tiny, had dyed black hair and a plastic face. We were all a bit shocked to see our 5 foot 6 hero in the flesh.

After a fun, chatty ten-minute interview I asked him to autograph a portrait of Rambo that had been entered in the Bathurst Art show in 1985. I had found the painting in a second-hand store, thought it was hilarious, and had given it to Merrick for his thirtieth birthday. Stallone happily signed it and then we had a photo taken with him holding the painting. We then got the picture framed and hung it next to the painting on the wall, and then took *another* photo of us standing next to the painting and the photo, and then got that framed and hung. It created a rather snazzy Sylvester Stallone triptych in the office.

As we were saying goodbye I told him how much I loved him in the cop–buddy film *Tango and Cash* playing opposite Kurt Russell. He lightly grabbed my arm and said, 'You know what happened with that film? I took the wrong role. I should have taken Kurt's role but we were trying to build this new image for me and have me wearing the glasses and being more sophisticated.' It was a surreal moment; it was like I was talking to a mate about his golf swing.

'Yeah, well Kurt's character did have all the jokes,' I offered.

'You're exactly right—he did have all the jokes! I don't know what I was thinking.'

Sly moved round like he was winding up to spend the next thirty minutes talking about the machinations of the decision-making process of a film that I'd rented once in 1994, and I was bang up for it, but unfortunately the film publicist ushered him out for his next interview.

It was pretty obvious that what he hated about *Tango and Cash* was not being the star of the film.

Watching the reaction of people in the office when famous people came to the studio was always interesting. David Hasselhoff was approached for more photos and autographs than anyone else, while more ladies found themselves accidentally walking past the studio to have a perv at Simon Le Bon and his mates from Duran Duran. I really liked the guys, particularly Simon, who, not realising the microphones were on, blurted 'What's the story here— can you say "fuck" or "cunt" on Australian radio?' The answer is, of course, not really, but he did get away with it because surprisingly we received no complaints.

When we were at Triple J we were delighted to have Adrian Edmondson and Rik Mayall from *The Young Ones* in the studio. Language restrictions are much looser at the ABC youth broadcaster, and we'd often let guests know in advance so we could have a more relaxed chat. If they dropped the odd expletive it wasn't going to have us taken off air. Rik Mayall certainly made the most of it because the opening of the interview went as follows:

Rosso: 'You loved them in *The Young Ones*, *Bottom* and *Filthy Rich and Cat Flap* and now they're here in Australia promoting their very funny new movie *Guest House Paradiso*. Adrian Edmondson, Rik Mayall welcome to Triple J.'

Rik: 'I don't mean to suck your cocks or nothing, but you can say anything you fucking want on Australian radio.'

I think my jaw is still on the floor.

With celebrities you get an entourage and strangely enough, sometimes the bigger the star the smaller the entourage. We were waiting to interview Matt Damon in the lobby of his hotel and you'd see him walk in alone with a takeaway coffee. But for every guy like that who is happy to ride the subway in New York, you'd get someone like Chris Brown, who would have twenty people wearing ridiculously oversized tracksuits, standing around all blinged up like Christmas trees.

You can't go past Dwayne 'The Rock' Johnson when it comes to over-the-top helpers. This one-time wrestler and star of *The Mummy* films came in one afternoon with eight people. He even had one of them check to make sure the bathroom was clear before 'The Rock' could go in for a tinkle. What did they think was going to happen? Was one of the sales guys going to jump off the top of cubicle two and nail him with a pole driver? The guy's almost 7 foot and as wide as a fridge. I reckon he was pretty safe in the Nova dunnies.

There's no doubt that Pink is very popular in Australia. She sold a gazillion tickets for her shows and now owns South Australia, apparently. She is totally engaging in real life and can make you melt just by telling you she likes your tie. Her minders can be a little over-zealous at times though. On her second-last tour we had a Friday afternoon interview with her at her hotel. I had just picked up my mum, who was up to stay from Melbourne for the weekend, and I thought it would be nice if she and her husband tagged along to watch the interview, even though they had no idea who Pink was. We popped them at the back of the room, set up the recording equipment and waited for Pink to rock up.

Just before she arrived, one of her minders came in, saw Mum and Michael at the back and ordered them to leave because Pink didn't do interviews with other people in the room. Mum was seventy-one, Michael had just turned eighty. What were they going to do? Jump off the top of cubicle 2 and nail Pink with a pole driver? They were just going to sit at the back of the room and watch me interview a musician. Thankfully, one of the people from Sony Music took Mum and Michael outside and got them a cup of coffee.

I'm sure if Pink had known that her people had acted in that way she'd be mortified. Any normal person would be. Not that Mum cared; when we left she couldn't believe that she'd got a free latte. God bless her.

I've always got the biggest buzz out of meeting the Aussies that I grew up watching on TV or film. I lined up for a beer next to Jack Thompson at the Byron Bay Blues Festival in 1999 and summoned up the courage to say g'day and when he looked at me, winked and said 'G'day cobber' I almost crapped my daks green and gold.

Merrick and I pretty much talked our way into being MCs at Bryan Brown's sixtieth birthday—a massive shindig that he combined with Sam Neil.

He took us out for lunch to chat through the event with singer Jenny Morris, who was pulling together the music for the night (guest musicians included James

Reyne, Bic Runga, and Neil and Tim Finn). After the lunch Mez was pretty keen to go home because we'd flown in from Melbourne and gone straight to lunch, but I was in the mood for a few more with Bryan. After he left, Bryan and I had one more, then I thought I wouldn't push the friendship and said I was going to head home too. Because I was going past his joint I offered to give him a ride home in the cab. We started talking about pubs in Balmain/Birchgrove that we both liked, and when he mentioned the Sir William Wallace, a great old pub that I hadn't been to in years, he suggested we might pop in there and have a couple more jars. It was unreal to walk into the bar and watch everyone say g'day to this Aussie legend. After knocking back three or four schooners, Bryan looked at his watch and realised he better head off home. He asked me what I was doing and I told him I was going to stay at the pub and wait for my wife to pick me up after she'd finished Pilates.

'That's stupid. Why don't you come back to my joint and I'll open a fucking bottle of wine and you can wait there!'

I was totally into the idea. We walked up the road to his house, this Aussie legend towering beside me as I dragged my suitcase behind me; it was like I was the kid in *The Shiralee*. Somehow, in the miniseries, I don't think that pair ever stopped to have a piss behind a Ford Falcon.

I'm not sure there's been a more interesting headline grabber in recent years than English comedian Russell Brand. The long-haired, bearded, rock-'n'-roll-styled funny man is a classic example of telling people you're a sex symbol enough times and sooner or later they'll believe you. Russell is one of the UK's finest comedians. We were lucky enough to support him for the Sydney leg of his 2009 stand-up tour.

After doing our spot at the first show, I watched his routine and thought he was brilliant. The next day he came into the radio station and did a special half-hour national show with us at 11am, which was fantastic. We only played a couple of songs, including one of his favourite Smiths songs, which I loved.

We hadn't spoken to him the night before because he'd arrived just before he went on stage. But he promised to come down early to watch our set and that we'd hang out.

The reality couldn't have been further from the plan. When we arrived at the Hordern Pavilion that night to do the gig, we went to find our dressing room, where everyone was setting up. I bumped into the tour manager and we were told that Russell was shooting some footage backstage and that they had us in a room on the opposite side of the venue—40 metres on the other side of the stage. It turned out our dressing room was also the sick bay that we had to share with the guys from St Johns Ambulance. A little bit surprised that we'd been quarantined, I asked whether we could have some beers. Five minutes later a minder returned with a green shopping bag and a couple of warm Crownies in it. Hello showbiz.

We had a good time doing our set in front of a crowd of around 4000 people, came off stage and Mr Brand was nowhere to be seen.

In 2006 we were accepted among the first group of Australians to be trained by former US Vice President Al Gore to present his slideshow of *The Inconvenient Truth*, his Academy Award-winning film on the effects of global warming.

It was an incredible experience to be part of the Climate Change Project run by the Australian Conservation Foundation.

The unique thing about the project is they choose people from all walks of life. Our group had farmers, scientists, schoolteachers, mining industry workers, doctors, corporate CEOs and low-rent comedians.

There was no doubt we were in awe of Al Gore. For the majority of the group this was the most famous person we were ever going to meet and his commitment to the environment is pretty impressive. Not so impressive was his then wife Tipper, who rocked up sporting a pair of Levis and a pair of Ugg boots. Crikey sport, just because you're in Australia doesn't mean you have to dress like an Australian!

The next day we met again in a function room in a Sydney office block. Gore took us across the road to the Botanic Gardens and we sat under a giant fig tree where he spoke about the importance of having a personal connection with the environment. It was incredibly inspirational. It was a sunny day and a slight breeze was coming off the harbour—a great reminder that we need to protect our fragile planet.

We also gained a big insight into the Australian character. At first almost everyone in the room was reverential towards Al. The questions were timid and extremely polite but as the day wore on and he tirelessly spoke, people became more comfortable with him and the truly egalitarian Australian spirit raised its funny old head.

People started pointing out the differences between the Australian climate and America's, correcting Gore on insignificant mistakes he was making about Australian geography, and bogging him down with pointless anecdotes about whatever small region of Queensland they were from and the raffles they'd held to raise environmental awareness. For most of us it was wincefully painful to watch this bloke who'd been on his feet for close to seven hours suddenly have to cop a barrage of useless questions and explanations from a few well-meaning but frankly annoying individuals.

It was apparent poor Al was at breaking point, the day had to be wrapped up so I decided to do something about it. I raised my hand and Al glanced at me with some dread as he nodded to me to go ahead. Getting to my feet I said, 'Al, I'd just like to say you're a fucking legend, mate'. There was silence in the room and I thought, Oh my God, I've just called a former vice president of the United States a fucking legend! This isn't good. Thankfully he smiled, then laughed and the whole room gave him a standing ovation.

When the day was over, I found myself in the lift with him and he thanked me for my gesture.

Not long after the training, I gave a talk on global

warming and climate change for staff from the Virgin Group. The plan was for me to give my talk and then Richard Branson would come out in a panda suit and tackle me. He'd then whisk off the panda head and reveal himself to the crowd. This sounds very much like I'm recalling a weird dream: 'I was standing there and a panda attacked me, but it wasn't really a panda, it was Sir Richard Branson!' Everything went according to plan and the crowd went berserk.

There's no doubt Branson's a very charismatic man. Can you imagine any other boss for whom people would line up for a photo and an autograph? Maybe Bill Gates, Steve Jobs and Barack Obama, but I think you get the drift. At work functions, employees are supposed to sit around drinking the boss's free booze and shit-canning them, not sliding up to them in a short dress for a photo.

I've got to get me an airline.

One of the great things about working at Nova was when they let us write our own television commercials. I'd always loved those jingles like Meadow Lea's 'You Ought To Be Congratulated' or the 'Brian Told Me So' campaigns Channel 9 did for its news bulletins in Melbourne and Sydney. So when we had the opportunity to do an ad for the radio show I jumped at the chance to knock up a bit of a piss-take. With the help of my old muso mate Hursto we wrote a jingle that was going to stick in people's heads for quite some time, and 'We Really Really Love Sydney' was born featuring the following rather stupid lyrics:

We really really love Sydney
We really really really love Sydney.
From Penrith to Panthers
Cronulla to the Shire
We love it so much it sets our hearts on fire.
Sydney, we really, really, really love Sydney
We really, really, really love Sydney.
We love it so much it hurts.

The truly ridiculous bit is that the Panthers leagues club is actually in Penrith and Cronulla is in the Sutherland Shire. After recording the jingle we went about gathering all our people. To make it look old school we knew we needed as many people singing along as possible so we enlisted the help of council workers, some police, a couple of celebrities in the form of Tom Williams and Laurie Daley and—the ace in the hole—then Premier

Bob Carr. Somehow we managed to talk him into coming down to the Opera House, putting on a hard hat, and standing there with a fake set of plans to hold on to while we pointed off to the horizon as if all three of us were planning a city on the move.

Just as we'd finished that scene someone from the Opera House came out to see whether we'd gained permission to film there. They are very particular about who can use one of the great buildings of the world and they often like to charge a rather large fee. Of course we hadn't bothered, so when quizzed we said, 'Bob said it was okay!' and pointed at the premier. As soon as she made her way towards him, we grabbed the cameraman and the sound guy and fucked off quick smart.

Of course one good turn deserves another and we got a call from the premier's people a couple of weeks later asking whether we would host his testimonial dinner to celebrate his ten years as premier. We obviously couldn't refuse the star of our new TV commercial so off we went to his tribute where they sold tickets for a few hundred bucks a head to fill the ALP's coffers. Bob was in brilliant form when he got up and straight off the bat quipped, 'It's not like the ALP to turn my big night into a grubby fundraiser!'

One of our roles on the night was to go round and hold the microphone for the speakers, who included all the state Labor premiers, except for the premier of Tasmania, who was there but wasn't included. Former Prime Minister Gough Whitlam was also there and it was a surreal experience to hold a microphone while he spoke in typical Gough style. I had been asked to keep an eye on the then Opposition Leader Kim Beazley's speech and wrap him up if he went on for more than a couple of minutes; apparently he was notorious for icing a room. When he pulled out a dozen sheets of notes I knew we were in for a punishing speech. After six minutes of kneeling in front of him while he sat at his table holding a microphone in front of him, one of the organisers caught my eye and gave me the wind-up sign. Looking for a way to wrap him up I pulled my phone out of my pocket and said, 'Sorry Kim, Kerry O'Brien from *The 7.30 Report*'s on the phone. He wants you to wrap it up.' Everyone laughed and he lost it and grabbed the microphone out of my hand, pointed at me and screamed, 'I know where you live, buddy'. Which is ridiculous because even though he was the Opposition Leader, he really didn't know where I lived. Silly Kim, it was at that moment I knew that he was Captain Cranky and he'd never be prime minister.

15

The meet and greet

I don't think there's anything that bands despise more than the meet and greet. Normally requested by the record company, this involves the band trotting out before or after the show to meet a few 'fans'. These 'fans' tend to be a smattering of competition winners, radio program directors, tour sponsors, celebrities, plus a sprinkle of assorted journos, hangers-on and anyone who needs to be sucked up to or placated.

It is always an awkward experience. Picture this: Chris Martin from Coldplay with a big fake smile, getting squeezed on the arse by a pissed TV exec's wife while a junior from the record company tries to work out how to use the digital camera. Slightly to the side is the rest of the band looking cranky, knowing full well that the star-struck crowd have no idea of their names and really only want a photo with the bloke that roots Gwyneth Paltrow.

My old boss had dozens of these pictures on his office wall. They were obviously fantastic conversation starters: 'Yes, that's me with Darren Hayes from Savage Garden. What a lovely bloke!' and 'Yes, that's me and fifty other people standing there when the Stones stopped for ten seconds, muttered something about taking Baby Boomers to the cleaners with overpriced tickets and then fucked off to New Zealand'.

This is the problem with meet and greets—you seldom get a photo with just you and the band. This is because the artists would rather have a rectal examination with an unlubed Gibson Flying V guitar than do these things. To ease their pain they pile as many people in the photo as they can so it's over quicker than you can say, 'Poo! Bono farted!'

My all-time favourite picture featured another ex-boss in a group shot with REM. In the heat of the moment he put his arm around a rival from another radio station and then actually forgot to put his arm around guitarist Peter Buck. Seriously, how can you fucking forget to hug the band?

I did get a kick out of going back stage to meet David Bowie (see how I have suddenly made it sound way more cool?). He had done a fantastic two-hour show, despite going a little heavy on the new material, and as always was dressed impeccably, on this occasion sporting a stylish white suit.

After waiting around in the bowels of the Entertainment Centre, I was devastated when he arrived. Gone was the suit and in its place the most hideous, oversized orange Mambo dad shirt I'd ever seen. You know those ones that fifty-year-old blokes wear featuring a dog taking a shit on a Torana while it rides a surfboard that looks like a cactus. Why did the Thin White Duke decide to experiment with dressing like a Manly cab driver the night of my photo opportunity?

He of course redeemed himself by being utterly charming. When introduced he shook my hand, looked me straight in the eye, and said, 'Nice to meet you, Tim'. Entranced, I felt like saying, 'You had me at the shit shirt'.★

★ I didn't actually think that at the time, I made that up because
I thought it would be amusing to tie my story about meeting Bowie
into a pop cultural reference to the film *Jerry Maguire*. Was it successful?
Why not start a trend on Twitter to find out?

I love that photo of me with Dave, my ex-girlfriend and ten total strangers so much that I can't find the bin where I chucked it.

Another interesting backstage encounter was with former Beach Boy Brian Wilson at his Melbourne show. Sitting up the front with a keyboard, he mumbled his way through his Greatest Hits catalogue, barely hitting the keys aside from a spirited version of 'Row Row Row Your Boat', for which, incidentally, he relied on the autocue for the lyrics.

After the show Brian sat at a card table while we patiently waited to get our copies of *Pet Sounds* signed. Ahead of us in the line was a rather nervous fan who had three copies to be autographed, each to be personally made out to the name written on the yellow Post-it note stuck to the cover. When plonked in front of him, Brian Wilson ignored the request for individual dedications and mindlessly signed the Post-it notes instead of the albums! By the time I got to him, things had gone from bad to worse. When I congratulated him on the show, he looked at me blankly and promptly missed my CD sleeve and autographed the card table. Fun Fun Fun until the drugs took his marbles away.

Back in the day if a film had tanked in the States they would often rush the stars out here to see whether the publicity could pull a few million dollars before everyone realised it was a turkey. Australia is a pretty easy market to come and blitz in a two- or three-day visit. This gave rise to the view that if someone has come out to promote a film it must be a bag of shit. Obviously the internet has changed this because we can now instantly find out if the reviews have been good, bad or indifferent. This means that nowadays we see the stars and directors of films that could actually be okay.

Quentin Tarantino has made a couple of visits over the last years for *Kill Bill* and *Inglourious Basterds*. For the first of these visits he came in a pair of black tracksuit pants and some black dress shoes, making an interesting-looking man even more so in a part Hollywood, part homeless guy kind of way. When he wasn't dazzling us with his impressive knowledge of Australian exploitation/horror films from the 1970s and early '80s, he told us about his new-found love for internet porn and how he been locking himself in his room for days. I'd rather watch an ear being cut off by Mr Pink than have to think of that image again.

Jodie Foster is a true Hollywood star in so many ways. When she was out promoting a film called *Panic Room*, she had few minders, was relaxed, wore no make-up and chatted warmly and with incredible honesty. This was a woman who had been famous for most of her life but was down-to-earth and totally fascinating.

When I think about interviewing Charlize Theron, someone you would expect would leave a lasting impression, all I can recall is that she was wearing too much fake tan and wouldn't have looked out of place at Northies in Cronulla or The Grand Hotel in Frankston.

Sandra Bullock had a neat trick. Whenever she entered a hotel room to greet waiting journalists she would make herself a cup of tea and give a bit of 'How y'all doing', then sit down, not touch the cup of tea, before moving on to the next room to make herself another cup of tea that she wouldn't touch. The ruse was designed to make her appear normal, of course. Like we'd all go 'Shit-a-brick that sheila from *Speed* sure knows her way around a teabag. She's so normal that I'm going to go and buy the complete series of *Miss Congeniality* films on DVD!'

John Travolta was a strange bloke who was particularly fascinated by my hair. We were talking about Vinnie Barbarino, his character in the 1970s TV show *Welcome Back, Kotter* and he decided that my hair was exactly like

Vinnie's and started touching it. I don't know whether you've ever been patted like a labrador by that dude from *Saturday Night Fever*, but it feels pretty weird.

When Cameron Diaz, Lucy Liu and Drew Barrymore came out to promote *Charlie's Angels* they certainly knew how to keep the boys on their toes. Fun and flirty after the chat we asked them to record a bit as if we'd left the room and the microphones were still recording so they could talk about how awesome we were. Drew kicked it off with 'I like the one with the beard'. Then Lucy said something about Merrick being hot and then Diaz went completely over the top and said, 'I wonder if they've got a big cock!' Everyone exploded with laughter, especially the girls, and after bleeping, it became the most played radio promo of the year.

The next time she was in town there was no such saucy language because she and Toni Collette were flogging their new chick flick *In Her Shoes*. And there in lay our problem. I saw the film, which was described to me as a chick flick by the film company, and I agreed with them, but Cameron took offence at the term. As a rule I don't get into tussles over semantics with women with blokes' names but this was a hard one to stomach. Despite Toni actually disagreeing with her, Cameron staunchly argued that the film was for everyone—although it was about girls and had the word 'shoes' in the title. It seemed to be a very strange disagreement to have with a Hollywood A-lister. I wonder if she's seen *Sideways*, that action film set in the Napa Valley?

A visit to LA doesn't guarantee meeting such big names, unfortunately. We went over for the launch of *Californication*, a comedy drama featuring David Duchovny, who, incidentally, didn't appear anywhere near our rented studio despite being the star of the show we were promoting for Channel Ten. Due to the sheer number of channels in the US and because *Californication* screened on the cable channel Showtime, more people actually watched the premier of this very edgy show on its first run in Australia than they did in the States. We did get to meet the very funny Evan Handler, who's best known as Charlotte's bald husband from *Sex and the City*. He happily told us there were delays to the film version of the series because the producers weren't interested in paying the minor characters much money, despite a multimillion-dollar budget. He was candid in a way I'd not seen before or since.

To fill up the show on such trips, you find yourself taking anyone—and we did, including the totally unbelievable Dr 90210, a very camp but happily married cosmetic surgeon who showed us around his practice and was particularly proud of the before-and-after shots in his labiaplasty scrap book. Essential reading for any lucky visitor! Dr 90210 was so whacky that we had to have him on the show when he came to Australia in 2009. He certainly pushed the limits of breakfast radio with his anatomical descriptions. He also led me into a line that has come back to haunt me. When he started talking about all the beautiful young hostesses that work for Qantas, I quipped, 'You obviously haven't flown domestic then'. I must say it's made for some very hurried justifications to some of our lovely older hosties on flights to Melbourne.

We also had the eye-opening experience of interviewing a couple of female porn stars. One of them was Candy, who allegedly had the biggest pair of breasts in the business—not a claim I was ready to dispute. Her friend, whose name thankfully escapes me, plonked down a couple of her DVDs in front of us and it was more than disconcerting to look at someone after you've just seen her close up to a rather large black man who I presume wasn't her husband.

They were both in their early forties and caked in bronzer and make-up, and Candy happily talked about the multiple breast enlargements that had left her with a

12ZZ chest or something equally ridiculous. We were also filming the interview for the website and just before we started, Candy's friend popped off to the bathroom. Halfway through the interview, when our cameraman got a flash he wasn't expecting, it appeared that she'd used that opportunity in the bathroom to take off her undies. After we'd finished she toddled off to the bathroom and put them back on. Nobody was game to ask why she had done this. When it was time for Candy and friend to leave (it was my hotel room we were using) I remembered some great advice we were given when we travelled to East Timor to entertain the troops: 'If the locals look a bit manky and they want to shake your hand, just wave at them to be on the safe side.' Four people happily waved goodbye to our X-rated friends.

MORE STUFF

STU

FF

How to bring a bit of celebrity into your own life

Do you want a little bit of show-business magic in your life? Well, try these on for size:

Leak your own sex tape

Sex tapes have been incredible for the careers of celebrities such as Paris Hilton and Kim Kardashian, and they can do wonders for your profile too.

This is pretty simple, film yourself and then either post yourself on a website and email the link to friends and family, or to make sure people really see it, invite the neighbours over for a video night and then 'accidentally' show them the vision by mistake. To make sure they really know it's you, give them their own copy on DVD to take home with them. Before you know it, people will be whispering about you in supermarkets, avoiding eye contact in the street, and inviting you over for weird dinner parties.

Organise a photo opportunity

Feel the adrenalin of being pursued by the media by paying your kids to race out the front of your house as soon as you get home and shove their Sony Cyber-shot in your face. To make it more authentic wrestle your seven year old to the ground, then stamp on the camera and yell, 'Get off my property before I call the police!' You could also ring your local paper and tell them you've just come back from a trek around Borneo for a non-existent charity or won the world aerobics championships. Most likely they will be round in no time to take a photo and write a story.

Act like a star

Most kids who ask for autographs don't actually know the stars they are approaching. I once met a bloke who asked Kamahl to sign his cricket bat because he thought he played for the West Indies. So if you rock up to the golf or the tennis, dress appropriately; you could find yourself signing autographs for hours. You only need one kid to ask and they will all come running.

News travels fast

If you really want to feel the power of fame among your peers, create a hoax death. Celebrities like Russell Crowe, Paris Hilton, Frank Sinatra and Sir Paul McCartney have all been the subjects of premature death rumours. Pick either yourself or a friend and put the following post on Facebook: 'Oh my God, did anyone else hear that Stuart's been killed in a light plane crash?'. If you want to make it more authentic add someone famous who has *really* been the subject of a death hoax into the mix. For example, 'I just heard that Jodie was killed in a freak roller coaster accident in Disneyland. You won't believe it, but William Hung from *American Idol* was killed too!' The fun comes when Jodie emails everyone to reassure them that she's working in Craigieburn, has never been to Disneyland, and doesn't even watch *American Idol*.

Change is as good as a holiday

Really want to look like a celebrity? Take a picture of a meerkat to a plastic surgeon in Thailand and pay them 200 bucks US to make you look like the weird little animal. Come home and wear a T-shirt that says, 'Yes, I've gone too far', just in case people don't get around to commenting on your appearance.

Jail time

Get a plastic bracelet, place it around your ankle, stay at home on Saturday and Sundays, and you've got yourself some old-fashioned celebrity weekend detention. If you want to go the whole hog, find one of those weird American retail sites that sells treadmills and clothes for dogs and buy a collar that will give you an electric shock if you go beyond a certain perimeter. Wear it when you go out to get the papers in your undies, cross the line and roll around the ground screaming, 'Damn this home detention!' Instant celebrity.

Sleep with the hired help

Nothing will make you feel more like David Beckham than sleeping with the nanny or your personal assistant. Unfortunately most people don't have either and sleeping with the babysitter is a big no no. This leaves more viable alternatives like your electrician, meter reader or in a worst-case scenario one of those weird travellers who sell bad paintings door to door.

Adopt a child

Getting to Africa or Asia to adopt a kid like Brangelina or Madonna is expensive and impractical. I mean, you have to pay to raise those kids for at least the next twenty years.

If you are Caucasian and really want to get the United Colours of Benetton look going on, get your children to befriend some kids at school from different ethnic backgrounds. Check them out for cuteness, and then organise an outing for you and a least two of the kids. Then you can spontaneously say, 'Hey kids, lets all get matching camo cargo pants and then we can go to Maccas!'

While the kids are stuffing their faces, tell complete strangers that dressing the children the same helps them bond and that adopting is the least selfish thing you've ever done in your life. This works best if you have boys and you make them grow their hair long like girls.

Flash

Nothing will make you feel more famous than showing more flesh than you need to. Next time you go to parent-teacher interviews don't wear any undies, park the car right out the front and expose yourself to fellow parents, teachers and the principal. Smoking!

Live beyond your means

Even celebrities forget that nothing lasts forever (not even the cold November rain). So why not buy a helicopter that you can't afford and then go bankrupt and be forced to sell your clothes to your neighbours? It's so very Hollywood.

Dress inappropriately

Take a leaf out of Madonna's book and start wearing a leotard on a daily basis as soon as you're over fifty. It works best if you're making a video clip, but popping down the street to buy some Yoplait will do just fine.

Become a brand

Unleash your inner Thorpie and lend your brand to a few things around the neighbourhood. Knock up a new sign and rename your local park after yourself. You could also make your own labels for sauce and stick them over Dolmio jars at the supermarket. While you're there, why not offer to do an appearance on centre stage at the mall?

Walk the walk

Act the part and you're halfway there. Take yourself far too seriously, don't eat, talk about yourself in the third person or even make your own baby bump out of a whoopie cushion and before you know it you'll be feeling as insecure as the real celebs.

The complaints file

When you do comedy there is always a chance that someone out there is going to be offended or that you will upset someone. Some jokes are obviously offensive, some are not. Back in the late '90s Merrick and I were on tour in Western Australia and I did an interview with a newspaper in Bunbury during which I was asked where we had met. In response I told a rather tall story about meeting in a juvenile detention centre, which the journalist printed. For our next run of shows out west we showed a clipping of the interview as a joke on stage. Unfortunately, the journalist who did the interview happened to be in the audience on that first night, and after the show she barrelled up to us, guns blazing and deservedly pissed off. We apologised, then after a bit it was all fine.

One of the unfortunate outcomes of the marriage between comedy and commerce are complaints. If you do jokes and there are clients involved, things can often go pear-shaped.

After nine years of commercial radio, I'm sure there were some doozies, many I suspect we were never told about. But there were certainly a few we *did* hear about. One time we were having a discussion about a new gaming console and I remarked that a friend had told me on the weekend that, although the new product was fantastic, if you had the existing console you probably didn't need the new one. That little comment saw the manufacturer, who I didn't know was a client, pull $50,000 worth of advertising. Whoops!

The worst situation involved a major fast food company who spent MILLIONS of dollars on radio advertising. Our general manager pulled us into her office one day and explained how she had gone in to a meeting with this client in order to secure another two-year deal and had been played some tape from that morning's show.

The basic gist of the banter was about a Mexican-themed burger that this particular company pulled out every year or two. It came with a supposedly spicy sauce that we suggested was about as spicy as water. Of course the jokes flew thick and fast and we were having a right old time amusing ourselves and, one would hope, anyone who was listening at 6.15 on a Monday morning. The break ended with me saying, 'The brains trust at—having been rolling this shit out since the '80s.'

So there was the boss with abovementioned brains trust, who, in my defence, *had* in fact been rolling that shit out since the '80s, but who were not the least bit amused by our on-air conversation and were threatening to pull all their advertising.

Desperately trying to save what was emerging as a rather major situation, I stood by the tried and true defence of 'all publicity is good publicity', which went down as well as one of their underseasoned burgers. Not one to subscribe to that golden rule of business—never ever fill the silence—I went with my own golden rule: if there's a fire, why not pour petrol on it? So added: 'It's a storm in a teacup, call their bluff. What are they going to spend their advertising dollars on? Sky writing?'

The boss quickly ordered a shit sandwich for me to eat and booked us in for an appearance at one of their large stores as a 'make good', and then someone's PA had to investigate whether or not sky writing could be a viable alternative to radio advertising.

Once I was lucky enough to be the spokesperson for an item that you buy in a supermarket. One of the stipulations of the deal was that I was to go to their major distributor and stand in the car park and hand out samples of the product to the staff. After a few minutes standing around twiddling my thumbs waiting for someone to come down, I went inside and with the permission of the receptionist, Sharon, asked people to come down and get a free sample while making a few very tame jokes about the receptionist trying to touch me up, which were received with quite a bit of laughter.

Suddenly everyone piled down to the car park to get their samples; some of them even went inside and put on a jacket to pretend to be someone else to get double the freebies. Half an hour later we were done and we left and everyone was happy—or so I thought until the following email was forwarded to my manager:

Afternoon David and Andre,
I wanted to write a note to express my disappointment that Rosso commandeered the PA system and made some offensive remarks this morning. This has marred what was shaping up to be a great event and has turned an email, which should be thanking you, into one highlighting the disaster that eventuated.

The comments such as 'I've just had Sharon, now I want a man. Are there any horny man lovers here?' might be better suited to a bar environment, but in a workplace where we have our executives, external visitors and women present it has not gone down well at all as it was transmitted through the entire office. I have been chastised by Stan's assistant, Peter was in a meeting with Daniel when the first indiscretion took place (which I wasn't aware of), who wasn't impressed and several complaints have been made.

Unfortunately this is going to make future sampling unlikely.

Regards,

Paul Winstanley.

Not in my wildest dreams would I ever have thought that anyone would complain about that event. Austin Powers uses the word 'horny' in case anyone's forgotten. The weird thing is that the email could have easily read like this:

Afternoon David and Andre,

I wanted to write a note to express how inventive it was that Ross commandeered the PA system and made some hilarious remarks this morning. This has turned what was shaping up to be an average event into a fantastic one, and has turned an email that would have been a polite thank you into one of immense congratulations.

The comments such as 'I've just had Sharon, now I want a man. Are there any horny man lovers here?' were a complete smash in a workplace where we have our executives, external visitors and women present. It went down so well as it was transmitted through the entire office. I have been praised by Stan's assistant. Peter was in a meeting with Daniel when the first jokes took place and they were really upset that they missed the hijinks. Brilliant stuff.

We can't wait to do business again soon and everyone wishes that Rosso could come and work here full-time. Perhaps he could become CEO when Daniel retires in October? LOL
Regards,
Paul Winstanley

Both emails work well, but I must say I like the second one best.

Understanding Gen Y

Much has been made in recent years of the character traits of Generation Y. For many, their attitude in the workplace has been frustrating, especially to those of Generation X. But in order to understand Generation Y we also have to understand the main motivators for other generations. By understanding our differences, it's only then that we can understand our similarities and exist together. Let's first take a snapshot of these groupings.

Generation Dead

Born before 1925. This generation ate heaps of bread and dripping and aligned themselves with values like surviving the Depression and avoiding the Spanish influenza.

Really Old People

Born between 1926 and 1945, this generation can be identified by their love of fruitcake and their false teeth.

Baby Boomers

Born between and 1946 and 1964, they like The Eagles ... Heaps.

Gen X

Born between 1965 and 1981, this Nirvana-loving generation spent all their money partying and travelling in their twenties, and then spent their thirties being angry about not being able to afford property. They still value taking pingers in their early forties and trying to squeeze money out of their Baby Boomer parents.

Gen Z

Alive any time from 2001. This generation is saddled with the burden of knowing that their major job will be to fight the Terminators in the Rise of the Machines.

This leaves ...

Generation Y

This group (1982-2000) was the first to grow up with computers, the internet, microwave popcorn, the threat of global terrorism post 9/11, and Lady Gaga. In order to understand and communicate with them you have to get to the core of their beliefs and values.

Computers and the internet

Unlike Baby Boomers, who got all their information from the Dead Sea Scrolls and carrier pigeons, Generation Y solely uses technology for information. The internet is their primary source of networking and fact gathering. Social networking sites like Facebook, Twitter, Myspace and Dildoswap have become the major way Gen Y communicates. Many of them have lost the ability to speak to each other without the aid of an electronic device. Many parents frustrated by this find the best way to alert their children that dinner is ready is to wait patiently near the computer on Chat Roulette, hoping that their child may see them with their meal waiting on the table.

Politics

The struggle for Generation Y is that they didn't grow up watching the TV show *Benson*, so they have little idea of how the American political system works. The danger of global warming has emerged in their lifetime and this has become a major issue that affects the way they vote. The importance of a solar-powered GHD hair straightener has become the number one issue for Gen Y female voters.

Transport and fashion

Being the first generation to grow up with the affordable Hyundai Excel has changed the way cars are perceived. The so-called stigma of a young male driving a 'girl's car' is no longer relevant. Similarly, 'girly' drinks like Bacardi Breezers are regularly drunk by Gen Y males, and they will happily wear bright fluoro colours and their sisters' tight jeans. General practitioners have seen a sharp rise in males in their late teens developing slight vulvas because of this behaviour.

Sexuality

For a generation that has always had access to pornography online, sexuality is a far different proposition than for generations before it. They commonly use more than one position, leave the lights on and take off their clothes while having sex.

Marriage

Economic security has been a major factor in Gen Y returning to the old-fashioned notion of marriage. However, changes in technology and the rise of this so-called 'self-absorbed' generation has led to many young people choosing to marry their cat, their iPhone, a pair of Chanel shoes, or a photo of themselves dressed up as Hamish Blake.

The workplace

For the generation that was brought up with *Big Brother* the idea of a workplace has a far different meaning. Many Baby Boomer employers find that Gen Ys refuse to do certain tasks unless they are given tickets to the Big Day Out. Gen Ys don't believe in hard work, refuse to put in the hard yards, wear inappropriate clothes, use inappropriate language in the workplace and have unreal expectations of their career path.

Cries of 'If I'm not CEO by thirty, you can shove your job up your arse!' are met with disdain by bosses but they are powerless because Gen Ys are the only ones who can show them how to make Facebook work for their business.

Home life

Generation Y, unlike Generation X, will never ever leave home. Their grand plan is to take the home over and move mum and dad into a shed in the back garden. Many seek Development Approvals to turn the family home into apartments, leaving mum and dad as caretakers in the smallest apartments, while renting out the others and using the profits to travel the world or buy a Mercedes.

Personal image

For the first generation that grew up with Botox—plastic surgery and Southern Cross tattoos being the norm, the desire to change their body is high on a Gen Y's personal agenda. Unlike Gen X, which embraced piercings, Gen Ys favour plastic surgery to look like famous people, aliens or the family pet. Hair extensions, teeth whitening and anal bleaching are commonplace. Such is the tribe mentality of Gen Y, that many friendship groups are having surgery so that they can look identical to each other.

Conclusion

Although many in this challenging generation have been able to harness the power of telepathy, the best way to try and communicate with them is still talking. Some people have found threatening to hit them with a broom if they don't answer is effective, but early studies show that this is a short-term solution and that many clever Gen Ys simply hide the broom so it won't happen again. The easiest way to co-exist is to visualise that they are almost real humans who have normal emotions and have some shared values such as enjoying watching *MasterChef* and breathing.

PART 7

16
Hey Dad

Both my parents are of Scottish heritage. My dad is the fourth John Macpherson Ross. The story goes that the first John Macpherson Ross actually spelt his name McPherson. He bought himself a watch and took it off to the engravers and they misspelt it Macpherson. He immediately changed his name to Macpherson because as a tight old Scot there was no was he was going to buy a new watch. Being frugal is a family trait, particularly on my mum's side.

When my brother had his twenty-first, Mum decided that buying ice was a waste of money so she just froze up a few ice cream containers full of water and used them to keep the drinks cool. Family holidays always brought on particularly frugal moments when she swiped the sugar cubes from motels to crush over the Weetbix later. The best moment was when we were about to cross the NSW–Victoria border and Mum made us get out of the car and eat a whole bag of apples rather than throw the fruit in the bins.

The old man is a funny bloke and a natural performer. As a kid I loved watching him perform on stage with the local amateur theatrical groups and it's obviously the reason I ended up on this funny old career path.

He was particularly good playing Bayonet, one of the drunks in the Jack Hibberd play *Dimboola*. In the musical *South Pacific* he played quite a good American Sailor. In the big number 'There is Nothing Like a Dame', Dad's wonky knee got the better of him. When he went down on one knee for the big deep-voiced 'There is absolutely nothing' it gave him such pain that the whole audience saw his face screw up as he mouthed the words 'Oh fuck!' My brothers and I laughed our heads off. What made it even better was that it was pensioner night.

Musical theatre was certainly on his brain when he

bumped into a woman he thought he knew at Bunnings one Saturday afternoon.

'Excuse me, didn't I do *Paint Your Wagon* with you?'

'No I don't think so.'

'Are you sure, maybe it was the *Student Prince*?'

'No I'm sorry, it wasn't me!'

Puzzled he walked off only to suddenly realise he'd been talking to Lindy Chamberlain.

Just before Dad's seventieth birthday I decided to take him on a trip. For years he'd always expressed interest in going to Easter Island, where the Moai, the large, ancient rock statues, have made the small, remote Pacific island famous. It's one of the most isolated places in the world, lying over 2000 kilometres from its two closest population centres (Tahiti and Chile).

We had a superb time driving round in a small Suzuki and checking out the historical sites. Because of Easter Island's isolation, you can be at any one of the many sites of these enormous statues and be the only person there. There are no shops, no hawkers trying to sell you souvenirs. Time after time we'd be completely alone, able to contemplate the enormity of humanity's achievement in complete silence.

There is a large dormant volcano on the south side of the island called Rano Raku. Dad and I walked around the top of the rim of the volcano until we arrived at a path that lead down, giving us a glimpse of the quarry where these gigantic statutes had been carved out of the rock. Almost half of the Moai on the island are still at the quarry, either never moved or still lying half-carved in the rockface. For Dad and me the experience was unforgettable.

With limited choices for dining we found ourselves eating at the one restaurant the whole time we were there, mainly because the food was pretty good but also because the waitress was rather cute. After six hours of sightseeing on our second-last day, Dad was tired and decided he didn't need any dinner. On the other hand, I was starving so I took my book down to the restaurant, ordered some fish, a bottle of wine and started reading. Half an hour later an American couple turned up and ordered some dinner. They heard me trying to flirt with the waitress, who spoke as much English as I spoke Spanish, and asked me to join them. They'd spent the last three weeks in South America and had pretty much spoken to no-one but each other for all that time and so were keen for some different company.

We chatted away while I kept half an eye on my friend, the waitress—that is until her hunky boyfriend turned up on a motorbike. When we finished dinner, the Americans and I got a couple of bottles of wine and went back to their hostel and had a few more drinks with a pair of Kiwi blokes who were staying there too. I can't remember how I managed to find my way back to the hotel but I did wake up with bruises over my legs from where I fell over a stone wall while taking a short cut through a paddock.

The next morning, with some fried eggs and toast in my belly, Dad and I got in the car again and took one more look at some of our favourite sites before it was time to head to the airport for our mid afternoon flight. On our way to drop off the hire car I spotted my new American friends walking along the road. I stopped to say 'G'day' and to introduce them to the old man. They were surprisingly frosty and as we drove off I tried to work out what I'd said to them the previous night that might have offended them. Nothing sprang instantly to mind and it wasn't until we were on the plane headed back to Tahiti that I realised what had happened. Being Captain Easter Island I'd told them that I'd show them around the sites in the morning and that I'd collect them from their hotel at 7.30. Deep in the haze of cheap Chilean red, I'd completely forgotten and they must have been sitting around waiting for me to turn up. No wonder they were frosty.

Not showing them around certainly didn't worry Dad—he'd had a great trip.

17
Centre link

I recently thought it would be a terrific idea to have a change in career. After some soul searching it dawned on me that, after eleven years of television and radio, basically being overpaid to do stuff all, I was perfectly qualified for a job in the public service. So after two minutes of flicking through the Saturday papers I stumbled on the following advertisement.

☎ 13 22 43   mycareer.com.au   31

MEDIA ADVISER

Deputy Prime Minister
Minister for Education
Minister for Employment
and Workplace Relations
Minister for Social Inclusion

JULIA GILLARD

Applications are invited for the above position.

Government Media Advisers play an important role in the development and implementation of Government communication strategies.

This position would suit a highly motivated person, preferably with several years experience in journalism or a related communications discipline and experience in the development of and implementation of communication strategies. Knowledge of government and parliamentary processes would be an advantage.

The position is offered under the *Members of Parliament (Staff) Act 1984* and conditions are outlined in the *Commonwealth Members of Parliament Staff Collective Agreement 2006-2009.*

A salary within the range $93,799 - $114,916 pa will be determined commensurate with relevant skills and experience. In addition, an optional allowance of $18,678 is payable. A probationary period of three months will apply. Employment is conditional on the granting of security clearance at the required level.

Applications setting out details of experience and the names of two referees should be forwarded to: **janine.robb@dpm.gov.au**

Applications close on Friday, 12th February, 2010.

For further information please contact **Janine Robb** on **(02) 6277 7320.**

I decided it was exactly the new challenge I was looking for. I could spank this job and work Julia G's profile into the stratosphere. Here's my application.

Dear Janine,
I thought I'd have a crack at being a media adviser for the deputy PM. Although my substantial career in the media is enough to get me across the line for this position, just to do things by the book here's my comprehensive list of why I'd be awesome at the job:

1.   My brother has red hair. Growing up in a red–hair–friendly environment will give me the winning edge with Julia. I learnt to communicate with rangas from an early age and I am equipped with a bunch of fun, office-friendly nicknames like carrot top, bloodnut and Fanta pants.
2.   I don't hate Canberra all that much and I'm a roundabout specialist.
3.   I've got a radio in my car so I can listen to Question Time when I'm going down the street to get a chicken schnitzel sanger.

4. I have been on the telly a few times and I can tell Julia what the red lights on top of the camera mean.

5. I can read.

6. I have watched the mini series *The Dismissal* (geez youse fucked that up!).

7. I have a Frequent Flyers number. (I presume we'll be doing a few hours in the air, many on non-government jets?)

8. I got eighty-one for Politics in Year 12. If you don't believe me get ASIO to check it out.

9. I'm not afraid to put sunscreen on members of parliament.

10. I don't believe the rumours that she has a crush on Tony Abbott.

11. I can write BOOBS on a calculator. Not really a vocational talent but a ripper way of diffusing a tense cabinet meeting, for example, 'Hey Kevin, I know the states are refusing to come into line on health care reform, but look I can write BOOBS on a calculator'.

12. If push comes to shove I'm prepared to character assassinate Kerry O'Brien. I'm also

willing to bribe Laurie Oakes with Krispy
Kreme donuts.

13. I can carry four schooner glasses without
a tray; perfect for impressing grass roots
supporters and pissheads.

14. I can count to fourteen.

15. I am brilliant at ignoring emails.

16. I can fill in an item on a list with pretty
much next to nothing; okay, I'll paraphrase,
completely nothing, to fool speed-readers.

17. I hate tennis. (It's a Liberal Party sport
isn't it?)

18. Julia and I have heaps in common including
both having made appearances on *Are You
Smarter than a Fifth Grader?*

19. I can wear jeans on the weekend yet still look
smart if needed for a press conference, plus
as a stand-up comedian I'll warm the room a
treat for the deputy PM. Five minutes about
growing up in Frankston before she gets up
and she'll tear the room apart.

20. I'll probably be considerably cheaper than
someone with necessary skills to do this job
properly.

Mum had a Kingswood

And finally while I'm at it, I reckon Julia has taken on too many portfolios. Can I suggest she pulls it back a bit, looks after just the one, which will free up her time so she can put more energy into undermining the Prime Minister.

Looking forward to my superannuation.

Love Rosso

The end bit

In February 2010 I was watching late night TV in my room at the Andaz Hotel in West Hollywood contemplating my life. I'd finished up after eleven years of daily radio and my wife Michelle and I had headed to Palm Springs for Modernism Week to indulge in my passion for mid-century modern architecture. We visited some incredible homes which had been opened up for the event, including Frank Sinatra's old house and the John Lautner-designed Elrod House that featured in the James Bond film *Diamonds Are Forever*. Nerding it up big time, we took architecture tours, attended talks and seminars and rode around on bikes taking photos of some stunning buildings. After a fantastic week, we headed to LA to catch up with some friends.

A few days earlier I'd caught up for a beer with my mate Jack, who's in television development at Comedy Central. I met him when Merrick and I had pitched a couple of unsuccessful show ideas a few years earlier, and we'd stayed in touch. I think Jack, who is a father of young kids, is more impressed that I know the Wiggles than with my comedy. Both he and another friend, Andie, like most showbiz types, desperately wanted me to take some meetings with some of their contacts while I was there. I was in holiday mode and not really interested, but they were insistent.

So off I went to meet with Mark, their friend at a major talent agency, who 'really wanted to meet me'. Sitting in reception on a large round couch, I couldn't work out whether *Entourage* had captured the industry perfectly or had inspired its behaviour as a succession of pint-sized, roly-poly Ari Gold clones walked in and out of the office having the most ridiculous over-the-top phone conversations.

After I'd watched their antics for a while, an assistant grabbed me and took me into the boardroom and told me that Mark would only be a few minutes. Mark arrived and we started with a bit of small talk about our mutual friends and then one by one another six people from different departments walked in, took a seat and all stared at me, waiting for me to weave some magic. Mark looked at me and said, 'So what are you hoping to do in LA?' Thinking I'd open up with a bit of fun I replied, 'I just want to make movies and shit!' Then for extra effect I clicked my fingers, pointed at them and added, 'You guys can make that happen can't you?' With a silly grin still on my face, I realised that they didn't think I was being funny as they all gazed at me straight-faced. The silence was broken when a portly chap with a goatee stood up and said, 'Sorry, we're wasting our time here. We're from the stand-up department; we thought you wanted to do stand-up, not films. We don't need to be in this meeting'. I then had to go through the torture of explaining that I was trying to be funny and that I was happy to explore any work opportunities and thankfully they stayed.

Worse was to come, though, when I heard the door open behind me. Thinking it was another agent who was joining the meeting a little late, I got up and turned round to shake his hand, only to come face to face with a Mexican guy who was bringing in a glass of water for the boss. I sat down again and stumbled through the next ten minutes as everyone explained their roles and what they did before they left, leaving Mark and me to talk about American politics and Russell Crowe. He believed that the reason Rusty had made it in Hollywood was because when he walked into meetings he had an 'I don't give a fuck' attitude that the Americans found appealing. Whereas I had more of an 'I don't have a fucking clue' approach to taking Hollywood by storm.

Mark was actually a very smart guy and to my surprise was genuinely interested in working with me. We shook hands in the lobby and as I walked past the large agency sign on my way out, I couldn't help saying to myself, 'What are you doing here, you little man from Mount Eliza? This is not your world.'

So that night, there I was, sitting looking out over the lights on the Strip and thinking about the future as I flicked through the channels on the TV, when I stumbled across Kathy Griffin's show *My Life on the D List*. Kathy is an actor and stand-up comedian who is probably best known as the redhead in *Suddenly Susan*. Her reality show tracks her life in Hollywood as she tries to drag herself up the showbiz ladder. This particular episode involved her coming to Australia so I thought I'd watch for a bit. A few minutes into the show I remembered that we'd done a phone interview with her before her trip to publicise her stand-up tour. Suddenly there she was on-screen mentioning that she was about to do some radio interviews in Sydney and before I knew it I was sitting there in Hollywood watching Kathy in her LA office on TV talking to us on speakerphone. I couldn't remember much about the interview other than we'd pre-recorded it one day after the show. Then when she said, 'I'm coming Down Under and I want some Aussie sayings to use', it all came flooding back. Kathy is a pretty outrageous comedian and her material can be quite explicit so you can have a fairly candid chat with her. Because it was a prerecord, and I thought she'd get a laugh from it I told her that Australians often greeted each other by saying 'G'day, cunt features', that old line from *Don's Party*.

Sitting there I thought, surely that part wouldn't be on the TV show? Leaning in to watch, I couldn't believe it! Not only was that piece of the interview shown, it was pretty much the only part of the interview they showed. The scene finished with her laughing and looking directly at the camera and saying, 'I can't wait to say "G'day, cunt features" to someone when I'm down there'. Despite them bleeping the bad word, it was still pretty full-on. The show followed her on the plane, showed her at

Mardi Gras, had some footage of her stand-up show and then previewed that she was going to interview Olivia Newton John.

After the break they showed Kathy going into a hotel room to meet Olivia and as she shook her hand she looked her in the eye and said, 'G'day, cunt features'. I don't know who was more shocked Olivia or me. I couldn't believe that I'd inspired Kathy Griffin to talk that way to one of our national living treasures. Olivia was obviously taken aback by this offensive greeting and Kathy justified it by saying that someone had told her it was a normal greeting in Australia. Thankfully, a flustered Livvy got over it and sat down and had a chat to her.

So there I was in America watching a woman I admire and respect, a woman who I stood up and cheered for when she was inducted into the ARIA Hall of Fame, being spoken to in a way she should never ever be spoken to. Because of me.

So what's next? I'm not sure but one thing's for certain: I'm going to track down Olivia Newton John and apologise and then I'll tell you what happened in my next book.

Acknowledgements

This book would not have been made possible if it wasn't for spellcheck, so big ups to the computer for that one.

On to the humans. Thanks to Mum, Dad, Stephen, Campbell, Gordo, Brooke, Nic, Michael 'Bulldog' Begg, Cahal 'Megsy' Meegan, and of course Ken 'Killer' Marsland.

To Claire, Renee, Siobhán, Robert, Susan, Karen, Lauren, Elissa, Caitlin and all the kind folk at Allen & Unwin.

And to Sean, Stacey and Craig at 22.

To Kit 'Hursto' Warhust, the best best man a man could ever have. Your support, faith and encouragement got me over the line yet again. Peter Holder, my Sydney

BFF: your guidance, kind words and professional advice will not be forgotten. Thanks buddy.

Finally to my beautiful wife Michelle, who slept next to me while I tapped away in bed most mornings, who set up a writing table that I barely used and remains my biggest fan xxxx to you.

book@timross.com.au